Julian's Cell

Other Books by Ralph Milton

Radio Broadcasting for Developing Nations
The Gift of Story
Through Rose-colored Bifocals
This United Church of Ours
Commonsense Christianity
Is This Your Idea of a Good Time, God?
God for Beginners
Living God's Way
The Family Story Bible
Man to Man
How to Write and Publish Your Church History
Sermon Seasonings
Angels in Red Suspenders

Julian's Cell

The earthy story of Julian of Norwich

And all shall be well and
All manner of thing shall be well
When the tongues of flame are in-folded
Into the crowded knot of fire
And the fire and the rose are one.

T. S. Eliot from *Little Gidding*

Ralph Milton

Editor: Michael Schwartzentruber
Cover & interior design: Margaret Kyle
Julian of Norwich cover illustration copyright © Cornwell ScribeWorks, Chico, CA; scribewrks@aol.com. Used by permission.
Cover calligraphy & interior illustrations by Don McNair. Copyright © 2001, Wood Lake Books Inc.
Proofreading: Dianne Greenslade

Northstone Publishing acknowledges the financial support of the Government of Canada, through the Book Publishing Industry Development Program, for its publishing activities.

Northstone Publishing is an imprint of Wood Lake Books Inc., an employee-owned company, and is committed to caring for the environment and all creation. Northstone recycles and reuses and encourages readers to do the same. Resources are printed on recycled paper and more environmentally friendly groundwood papers (newsprint), whenever possible. The trees used are replaced through donations to the Scoutrees for Canada program.
A percentage of all profit is donated to charitable organizations.

National Library of Canada Cataloguing in Publication Data

Milton, Ralph
Julian's cell
ISBN 1-896836-50-X
1. Julian of Norwich, b. 1343--Fiction. II. Title.
PS8576.I57438J84 2002 C813'.6 C2001-911619-5
PR9199.4.M54J84 2002

Published by Northstone
an imprint of Wood Lake Books Inc.
Kelowna, British Columbia, Canada
www.joinhands.com

Printed in Canada by
Transcontinental Printing

Dedication

To the Vancouver School of Theology Pilgrims
who introduced me to Julian,
1997 & 2000

After you have read *Julian's Cell*, you may want to explore her story and her spirituality a little further.

Reading her *Showings* can be difficult. Even Colledge and Walsh, the translators of the critical edition of her books, say that "Julian is hard going."

There is help on the way.

The Essence of Julian is my own modern, easily-read condensation and paraphrase of her book *Showings: Revelations of Divine Love.* It will be available in the fall of 2002, from Northstone Publishing.

Ralph's Resource Barrel at www.joinhands.com contains a number of other resources for those who want to continue their study of Julian.

Contents

Note: Excerpts from Julian's *Showings* as they appear at the head of each chapter and in the text itself, are the author's own paraphrase.

Preface

I was blindsided. I didn't see her coming or I might have ducked.

But there I was, sitting in a small, dreary little chapel off the church of Saint Julian's in the heart of the Norwich red-light district. I was trying, unsuccessfully, to meditate. Time seemed to compress. I had gone into the shrine where Julian's cell once stood, an hour before the bus was to leave. I had lots of time. Then suddenly Bev, my wife, was tugging at my arm. "The bus is leaving!"

Can most of an hour simply disappear? Strange that was, but more strange still was the commitment I knew I had made during that missing hour. As I walked to the bus, I knew I had pledged myself to learn from this mystical and mysterious woman. She had prayed for almost fifty years on that spot. Out of that prayer had come not just the first book to be written in English by a woman, but a powerfully inclusive spirituality that is still radical now in the 21st century. (She would have been astonished to learn that many 21st-century therapists regard her as their professional forebear.) As I stepped onto the bus, I knew I would not only get to know her and understand her teachings, I knew I would write about her.

Can a grey-haired Canadian male, a curmudgeonly Protestant liberal really get to know, much less understand, a 14th-century female mystic who spoke in a strange medieval dialect of English – whose images and metaphors and world view were those of the Roman Catholic late Middle Ages?

No. He can't. But neither can anyone else alive now, 600 years later. Far better scholars than I am have dissected her writings and offered many insights. They have helped us know her in one sense of the word. But they don't know her in the sense that you might know a person you live and work with.

The late Eileen Power, a noted medievalist, once wrote, "For history, after all, is valuable only insofar as it lives… It is the idea that history is about dead people, or worse still, about movements and conditions which seem but vaguely related to the labors and passions of flesh and blood, which has driven history from bookshelves where the historical novel still finds a welcome place."

Popular historian Thomas Cahill, in his *Hinges of History* series, points out that history is so often the chronicles of kings, the struggles of popes, the wars, the outrage, the cataclysmic events. "But history is also the narratives of grace, the recountings of those blessed and inexplicable moments when someone did something for someone else, saved a life, bestowed a gift, gave something beyond what was required by circumstance." He must have had Julian of Norwich in mind.

I am not a scholar. But I can do something many scholars can't. I can tell a story. I'm a spinner of yarns and I can sometimes make history live. The inner voice that commanded me to write about Julian of Norwich did not prescribe another scholarly analysis, which I'm not qualified to do anyway. There are many of those and most are excellent and have been enormously helpful to me.

My call was to tell her story in such a way that ordinary folks, the people Julian calls her "even Christians," can feel the breath of her spirit, and may be encouraged to learn more about her. I knew I needed to tell her story in a way that was accessible to tourists like me, who wander into the small shrine built on the site of her cell or who pick up one of the small booklets of quotations from her writings. I also wanted my book to be useful to those who read Julian for her radically inclusive, integrated teachings about a mothering God. Such a book would necessarily include the juicy circumstance and personality that more scholarly books omit.

Julian said almost nothing directly about herself or the times in which she lived. We know when she was born and approximately when she died. We know when she had her visions and when she wrote the "Long Text" of her book. Almost everything else we can say about her is by inference, but it is inference based on a high level of probability.

Julian saw herself as the medium, not the message. She handed down to us what she received from God. But many of us have discovered that when we find out more about the times in which she lived – times described by historian Barbara Tuchman as "the calamitous 14th century" – her writings and her teachings take on new richness and depth. And her story becomes much more evocative.

After four years of research and meditation, I sat down and watched my tale take shape before me on the screen of my computer. It is an imagined story about that strange, intellectual, enigmatic woman, whose name we don't know, but whom we call Julian of Norwich.

I immediately realized that the Julian who arose in my imagination was somewhat different than the Julian I had encountered in some of the books about her. For some writers, Julian was quiet, iconic. They found a woman who yearned for nothing but her time of prayer – who showed no profoundly human weakness, who needed no other human in her life. That kind of Julian was "not shewed me," as she would have said it.

Those other writers are not wrong. They came to Julian with different intuitions – different needs. Whenever we encounter people from the past who speak to something deep within us (such as the characters in the Bible, for instance) and we imagine what they were like, we create their personalities out of our own perceptions and needs. I freely confess – that's what I did with Julian. Unlike some other writers, I *know* I am being highly subjective.

Julian wrote out of a long, biblical tradition of storytellers who understood, somehow, that mere facts could never contain the wonder they felt in their souls – their intimate experience of God.

It was not Julian's knowledge of the Bible or the writing of the early church fathers that motivated her, even though some historians say she knew both well. She wrote out of her personal experience of the holy. That is why we call her a mystic.

Julian entered deeply into the experience of Christ's crucifixion, and that gave her the grace to speak to us in images and metaphors that leap across the centuries from her soul to ours. Her meditations on a mothering God and a mothering Christ convinced me that her own experience of mothering was deep, powerful and good, and therefore mothering would be an important theme in my story.

Julian was born in 1342, the same year as Geoffrey Chaucer, though I doubt they ever heard of each other. In my view, she was his literary equal, certainly not in terms of the quantity of writing, but in its quality. It is remarkable how well she handles her language when there were few (if any) models of literary English for her to learn from.

Given that reality, it is even more astonishing that her book is a literary triumph.

Furthermore, the depth of Julian's theology is astonishing, even though she probably had no formal training in this field. The contemplative monk Thomas Merton wrote, "There is no doubt that Lady Julian is the greatest of the English mystics. Not only that, but she is one of the greatest English theologians in the ancient sense of the word."

Julian wrote in the tradition of the great mystics: Hildegard of Bingen, Catherine of Siena, Bridget of Sweden (whom she mentions) and others. Most medieval writers, including these mystics, describe humans as being loathsome worms, totally undeserving of God's love and mercy. The church at that time preached a vindictive God who set up impossible standards and then rained cataclysmic punishment on humans for their failure.

To Julian the human creature is a treasure in the heart of God. We are of the same essence as our God, who reaches out to us in motherly tenderness, longing to be reunited ("oned") with us. We are not complete and God is not complete until that union takes place. It's hard to believe that such an open, eloquent, optimistic, joyful book could have been written in such a dark and painful time as the late 14th century.

This is not a book of history, although there's lots of history in it. Except for the little Julian tells us of her life, I have invented her story. It's a plausible story, based on extensive research around the circumstances, events, and people of her lifetime. While we have little in the way of facts about Julian's life, we have lots of documented history about the people, the events, and the culture of 14th-century Norwich.

We know quite a bit about people like Bishop Despenser, John Ball, Margery Kempe, and Maggie Baxter. However, except for Margery who tells us about her visit to Julian, we have no accounts of their interaction with her. But they certainly would have known about each other, and it is entirely possible that they visited Julian in her cell.

Even kings were known to consult anchorites. King Richard II visited an anchorite in London on his way to deal with the Peasants' Revolt of 1381. Julian was evidently a counsellor of considerable repute in Norwich. We know of two wills that mention her. Those intriguing possibilities are all a storyteller needs. So my account of their meetings is fictional but plausible.

Julian did have a maid named Alice, but we know almost nothing else about her. There is some evidence that she became an anchorite herself. The wonderfully earthy Alice that unfolded as I wrote about her has no historical basis whatever. It just seemed to me that an intellectual, spiritual giant like Julian needed a maid like Alice.

There are many theories and hunches about where Julian grew up, how she learned to read and write, whether or not she was a nun, when she became an anchorite, and how she lived her life in that enclosure. My story of Julian is an amalgam of those many theories, though I have fleshed them out with dialogue and action. By the way, if you wonder if it is possible for a person to teach herself to read the way Julian did, I watched a child do exactly that at the age of two.

Julian's Cell is not a book of theology, though every story that tells of humans encountering God is theology in one sense. Julian's faith is open, bright, and full of hope, and not at all like some of the stuffy tomes you may associate with that discipline.

Having said that, Julian's writings are sometimes very heavy going. In developing her character and dialogue I have tried to be faithful to Julian's deep and complex spirituality. Those familiar with her writing will recognize many passages – many phrases and ideas – from her *Showings* in the words I have her speak.

When all is said and done, this is a book of fiction. I am what Stephen King calls "God's liar…who can sometimes discern the truth that lives at the center of the lie." I believe my story to be truthful – in the sense that it faithfully and plausibly reflects the spirit and the lively faith of this remarkable person. It is true in the sense that all good fiction reveals the truth, even when some of the facts may be in dispute.

This is a story about a 14th-century woman who struggled to know and serve God, told by a 21st-century man who is struggling to know and serve God. If somehow this helps you in your struggle, and has you wanting to discover more about Julian's spiritual odyssey, my story will have achieved its purpose. (There are further resources suggested on page 223.)

We begin with a teenager and her mother. That teenager is the person we later come to know as Julian. We don't know what her real name was before she became an anchorite and took on the name of the church where she was enclosed. I've chosen to call her Katherine because it is the name of someone I love and because it was a name in use in Norwich during Julian's time.

Acknowledgments

This book has been as much a journey of faith as a literary exercise. And I have been profoundly enriched by the experience.

There are two people who have walked that journey with me. It sounds like a truism and a cliché, but it is nevertheless the case that the Reverend Beverley Milton, my mate of almost forty-four years, and my closest friend and colleague, Dr. James Taylor, brought their friendship, love, and professional competence into this book at every stage of the way.

I might not have been introduced to Julian at all if it had not been for two other friends from the faculty of the Vancouver School of Theology. Reverend Lynne McNaughton and Dr. Gerald Hobbs led a group of "pilgrims" who went from Canada to Britain to search for some of the roots of our faith. On that pilgrimage, we visited Julian's Shrine in Norwich, where that strange incident of which I tell in the Preface forged a mystical link between myself and Julian. But not before Archbishop David Sommerville had opened our eyes to the essential difference between a cell and a prison.

Three years later, after spending far too much money on books and far too much time on the Web, Bev and I returned to Norwich. Our way was eased by the kindness of Judith and Vince Gilbert and the hospitality of the nuns at All Hallows Hall, a guesthouse next door to Saint Julian's Church.

Our few short weeks in Norwich were delightful and productive because of the kind and helpful friendliness of so many people in so many ways. There were those who not only gave us directions, but walked part of the way with us through the delightful maze that is old Norwich. And the staff in the various libraries: The Norfolk Studies Library, the Norwich Cathedral Library, and the Julian Resource Centre operated by the Friends of Julian (see Resources on page 224) went the second and third mile to help me find the materials I needed.

Two new friends from Norwich deserve special mention: writer Sheila Upjohn whose excellent books are listed on page 223, and historian Martial Rose whose knowledge of medieval mystery plays and the carved bosses in the Norwich Cathedral was invaluable.

Dr. Michael Treschew of Okanagan University College was helpful in translating documents from Medieval Latin, and in providing useful information on the life and theology of John Wycliffe. Dr. Frank McNair, psychiatrist, helped me understand the strange mind of Margery Kempe, and Dr. Colin Partridge threw interesting light on Julian's illness.

After I had tried the first draft of *Julian's Cell* out on Bev and incorporated her suggestions, I sent the second draft to a group of family and friends to get their reactions. They were Reverend Dorothy Barker, June Burgess, Lois Huey-Heck, Don McNair, Kari McNair, Mark Milton, Grace Milton, Bonnie Schlosser, Mike Schwartzentruber, and Dr. James Taylor.

These friends and family were kind, but they were also brutally honest. Such comments were not always comfortable, but they were helpful.

Having incorporated their suggestions, I then faced a tougher jury. I asked six professionals, each with particular competencies related to this project, to read the manuscript and to offer criticisms and suggestions:

- Rev. Dr. Gerald Hobbs, Vice Principal and Professor of Church History, Vancouver School of Theology
- Fr. John-Julian, founder of the Order of Julian of Norwich, Waukesha, Wisconsin
- Reverend Lynne McNaughton, Chaplain and Director of Anglican Formation, Vancouver School of Theology
- Rev. Dr. Victor Shepherd, Professor of Historical Theology, Tyndale Seminary, Toronto
- Dr. James Taylor, author, editor, theologian, and Renaissance Man
- Sheila Upjohn, writer and author of several books on Julian, who has lectured extensively on the subject.

These folks were tough in their criticism and perceptive and analytical in their comments. None of them will be totally happy with the final product because often their suggestions were contradictory. That is in the nature of such an enterprise, which relies so much on the cooperation and good will of others.

My much loved son-in-law, Don McNair, did the illuminated letters, illustration, and map. Margaret Kyle designed the cover and book, and Mike Schwartzentruber, the editor, massaged the whole thing to make it much more readable. Their fine work speaks for itself.

Julian's Cell is a historical novel. It is fiction. In the final analysis, I take responsibility for the many weaknesses and biases it reflects. Insofar as it is helpful, plausible and truthful, thanks goes to the folks listed above, to whom I say a heartfelt thank you.

Timeline

Items in regular type are established historical fact. The items in *italics* are fictional.

1275–1299: Anonymous priest writes the Anchorites' Guide
133?: Richard Rolle writes English Psalter, *the first book Julian reads*
1337: Hundred Years War begins
1342: Katherine (Julian) born; Geoffrey Chaucer born
1347: Outbreak of cattle disease in Norfolk
1349: Plague reaches Norwich
1358: *Katherine married to Walter*
1359: *First baby born, Maud goes to Carrow*
1361: *Second baby born*
1362: *Phillip (Walter's father) dies. Katherine inherits book.* The children's plague. *Katherine's children and husband die. Katherine moves to Carrow Abbey.*
1370: Bishop Henry Despenser enthroned
1373: Katherine receives her Showings. Margery Kempe born
1374: *Katherine enters anchorhold, and becomes Julian**
1375: Julian writes Short Text
1377: Great Papal Schism begins – rival popes in Rome and Avignon
1381: Peasants' Revolt. *John Ball visits Julian.* Ball hanged.
1383: Despenser's "crusade" against schismatics in Flanders
1384: Wycliffe dies at Lutterworth
1384: Early version of English Bible completed
1385: Sheriffs given power to arrest and imprison Lollards
1393: Julian begins work on Long Text
1397: Bishops, led by Despenser, receive permission to burn Lollards
1401: William Sawtry, Norwich Lollard, burned
1413: Margery Kempe visits Julian: *Maggie Baxter visits Julian.*
141?: Julian of Norwich dies at age of seventy plus
1428: Maggie Baxter tried and found guilty of heresy
1436: Margery Kempe begins to dictate her autobiography to a priest.

* We do not know when Julian entered the anchorhold.

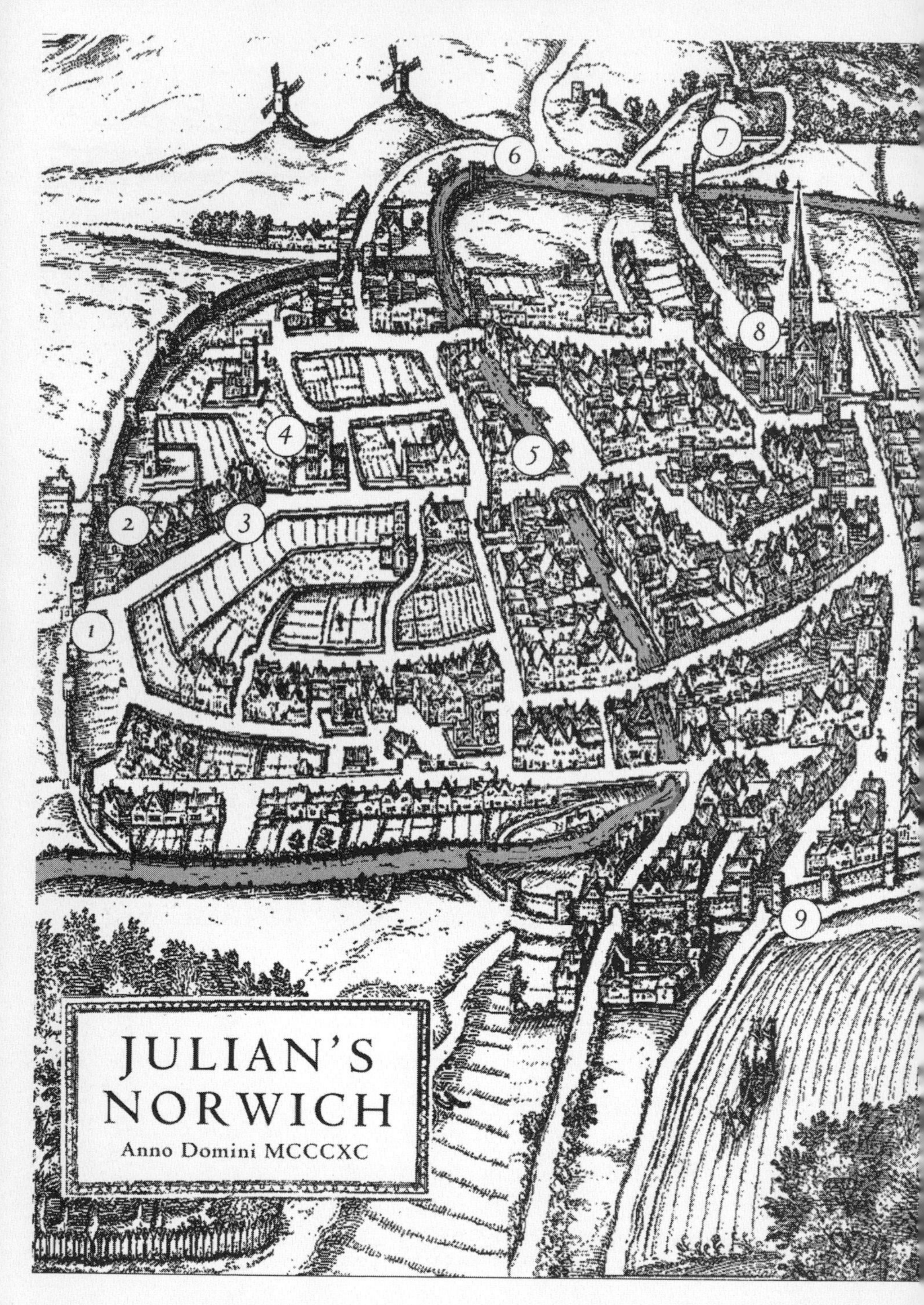
1
2
3
4
5
6
7
8
9
JULIAN'S
NORWICH
Anno Domini MCCCXC

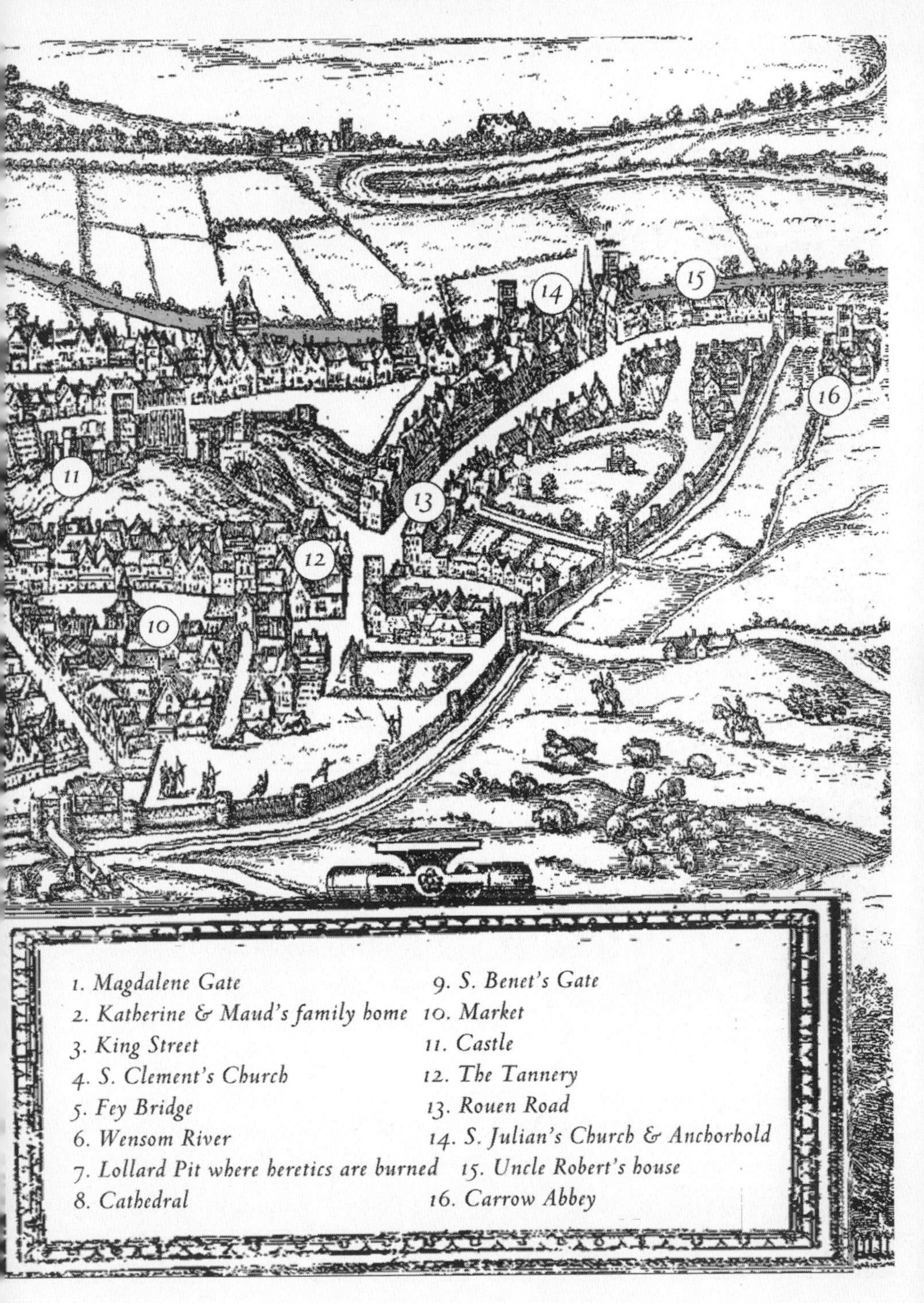
11
12
10
13
14
15
16
1. Magdalene Gate
2. Katherine & Maud's family home
3. King Street
4. S. Clement's Church
5. Fey Bridge
6. Wensom River
7. Lollard Pit where heretics are burned
8. Cathedral
9. S. Benet's Gate
10. Market
11. Castle
12. The Tannery
13. Rouen Road
14. S. Julian's Church & Anchorhold
15. Uncle Robert's house
16. Carrow Abbey

1358

After this God said,
"I thank you for your labor,
and for your service
when you were young."
And then my mind
was lifted up to heaven
where I saw God at home,
and God's house was full of servants and friends,
all of them at a feast
full of joy and laughter.

Spring is most beautiful, verdant, sensual, exhilarating, when lived through the body and spirit of a lithe, young, almost woman. Spring rain fresh on the grass. Blood-red roses scrambling their fragrance and their thorns over a half-ruined wall. Wildflowers dancing by the roadside. And on the cool spring breeze, the wholesome scent of plough horses from a nearby farm.

And a spring song – a song sung easily through the lusty red lips and from the blossoming breast of a fifteen-year-old almost woman soon to discover the man she hopes to love.

Summer is a comin' in,
Loudly sing, cuckoo!
Now grows the seed, now blows the weed,
The woods are fresh and new.
The ewe bleats for her lamb,
The cow lows for her calf,
The bull leaps, the buck farts,
Merry sing, cuckoo!
Cuckoo, cuckoo,
You sing so well, cuckoo!
Don't stop. Sing out! Cuckoo!

It was a fine, sensuous song to be singing on the way to your wedding. Well, not quite the wedding yet. She was going to her betrothal, to the home of her uncle who had arranged the marriage. He would introduce her to the groom. His name was Walter, that much she knew. A very ordinary name, she thought. But he would be tall and kind and handsome and loving. She refused to let herself think that Walter might be old, ugly, and mean.

"Stop that caterwauling, Kate!" snapped Maud, the bride's mother. "You'll be married in a few weeks, then you'll pay your marriage debt in the filthiness of sin. And that'll have you heavy with child and all the pain and sorrow and heartbreak that children bring. You'll stop singing soon enough."

"Will Walter and I love each other?" Kate pleaded. "Did you and papa love each other, Mama?"

"It doesn't matter. Be silent!"

Maud and Kate, with her younger brother, Thomas, lived just inside the Magdalene Gate in the north end of Norwich. They lived almost in the shadow of the new city wall, completed about the time Kate was born in 1342. There were open fields of fresh green barley between their home and wool shop in the borough of Ultra Aquam and the more populated areas of the city. Low, deep green hedgerows full of bright roses dancing to the sun's promise surrounded the fertile fields. They walked past Saint Clement's Church where they attended each Sunday, through rows of narrow shops where artisans lived and died, plied their trade and sold and bartered.

Maud and Kate crossed Fye Bridge over the muddy, winding Wensum River. The Wensum and the defensive walls of Norwich in 1358 defined most of the pear-shaped city. On the eastern side, the Wensum formed a natural barrier against attack. Just north of Norwich Cathedral, the walls took up their protective duties again. The Wensum veered to the west just north of the cathedral where it served as a boundary between the districts called Ultra Aquam and Westwyk.

In the northwest corner of the city, just past Saint Benet's Gate, the river lazed its winding way toward the east coast of England. Not far from the coast, the Wensum joined the River Yare, and flowed into the cold North Sea at Yarmouth. It was a short but sometimes risky sail from Norwich across the Channel to Flanders – easier to get to than London.

The easy contact with Flanders in the wool trade gave Maud and the other wool merchants of Norwich their livelihood. She bought raw wool from the landowners who ran the sheep, cleaned it, had it spun into yarn, then shipped it across the Channel to the Flemish weavers. That wool trade made Norwich a wealthy city, second only to London in size and importance. Maud and the other wool traders worked easily with the Flemish merchants and seamen. The Frisian (Saxon) invaders of the fifth century had brought their lowland Germanic tongue to England, and the Norfolk dialect was almost understood across the Channel in Flanders.

Maud was part of a growing population of middle-class crafters, artisans, and shopkeepers. A prosperous marketplace brought traders and buyers together in the centre of the city. The market was watched over by the looming castle of the Earl of Norfolk. It was a bustling city, but even so, it was not much more than a half-hour walk from the Magdalene Gate in the north to just outside the southern gate where sat Carrow Abbey, the largest convent in the county of Norfolk.

Kate loved the city smells – well some of them, anyway – the hot, savoury pork pies; the clean scent of soft soap; the sweet, almost pleasant, almost nauseating smell of fermenting ale. She and her mother stopped to wonder at the hulk of Norwich Cathedral dominating the city.

Kate could not remember ever being inside the cathedral, but she had vivid memories of standing in the cathedral close on Corpus Christi day. Her younger brother, Thomas, and her bosom friend, Annora Parke, had gone with her to watch the Mysteries every spring. All the craft guilds assembled near the cathedral to dramatize the origins of Christianity, each guild acting out one small part of the Bible's holy story, from the fall of Lucifer (which isn't really in the Bible) to the Holy City of God described by John in the Book of Revelation.

It seemed to Kate that almost everyone in Norwich crowded into the cathedral close to watch this annual event, though of course that would have been impossible. The three children pushed and struggled their way through the crowds of preoccupied adults to find a place where they could see and hear the dramas.

This was no casual entertainment. For Kate and Thomas and Annora and all the others watching, this was history. It was *their* story – the way things happened. These sacred, sometimes bawdy dramas generated many a lively discussion over a cup of ale at the nearby, hundred-year-old Adam and Eve Pub.

It was the first play in the cycle of Mysteries – the fall of Lucifer – that pressed itself into Kate's consciousness and dreams: the great, gaping, painted wooden jaws of hell opening to devour the fallen angel, and the stench of hell that belched from that great maw; the stink of stale urine and rotting feces. The honour of presenting this odorous opening scene went to the tanners, or barkers as they were called. Their craft was noted for its stink.

Walking with her mother along dusty King Street past the cathedral, Kate remembered how one year when she and her friend Annora were ten years old, they watched the crucifixion of Christ, presented by the Carpenters' Guild. Kate stood between Thomas and Annora, holding their hands tightly, feeling the revulsion rising inside her. Pale and shaken, Kate walked home unsteadily with her brother and friend, but stopped to steady herself near a hedgerow of roses. The scent came up strong, sweet, revolting. She heaved and retched and crumpled into the rose bush. The thorns scratched and tore at her skin. Annora pulled her bleeding friend from the thorns, then saw Kate and her brother safely home.

The crucifixion drama left Kate shaken and confused. She had often wondered, as she prayed before the crucifix in church, whether she, the child of a common wool spinner who had no large fortune and no father, might enter that passion, might live with Christ that cruel death, might live the prayer-filled life of a sainted nun. She and Annora dreamed that dream often, in their neighbourhood just inside the Magdalene Gate. But then her dream faltered, for if she could not watch a staged crucifixion – if she cried from the cut of a few rose thorns…

Still, Kate and Annora dreamed, as only ten-year-olds can dream, of how they would have great visions of the risen Christ, of how they would become virgin saints and all the world would beat a path to their doors. There were only two dreams available to pubescent girls. Pious glory as a nun, or the even less likely dream of a gallant knight in shining armour who would be smitten by her beauty and carry her off to live happily ever after in a magnificent castle on a hill.

Kate and Annora had both dreams, of course. But for Kate the fantasy of sharing with Christ his cruel death matured into a prayer, and grew within her each Corpus Christi day. On her knees in Saint Clement's Church, she prayed that she might know the pain and horror of the crucifixion, though often she would wonder why she would want to do that. Perhaps it was because she so often also had nightmares about the revolting stink of hell's red, gaping jaws.

Just past the cathedral, to their right, loomed the Earl of Norfolk's enormous castle. Her mother turned off King Street, leading Kate along the reeking offal of Cattle Market Street, and through the putrid pungency of the fish market.

Kate wanted to run now, because the astringent smells began to assault her nose and water her eyes, but her mother slowed her pace and searched the shop fronts as if looking for something or someone. These were the tanneries. Kate shuddered and her eyes watered in the acrid stench of cow and sheep hides being scraped and soaked in dung and urine. Memories of the mystery plays and of this stomach churning smell sent the fear of Satan shuddering through her body.

Maud caught her daughter by the sleeve. "That's his father's place," she said, pointing to a narrow, dingy shop with several tanned hides hanging in the open front. Then Maud moved quickly on, ignoring the look of horror on her daughter's face.

Maud almost ran now – her jaw clenched, her face set and grim and angry, her daughter running to catch up. It was the smell that tightened up Maud's face, the stink of rotting flesh that brought sudden, stabbing memories of death. Past the butcher shops they raced, where the guts of cows and sheep were squeezed and emptied into open sewers, where blood and waste oozed down the gutters, rotting, until a heavy rain would wash it down into the sluggish river. A large black rat scuttered across the street in front of them.

It was the plague that turned her mother into stone – the pestilence that killed her father. Killed her brother. Killed her two sisters. All this when Kate was only six. She hardly remembered. She wished she remembered less. Imprinted in her mind was the smell – the gut-tightening stench of death – the picture of her haggard mother dragging her father's almost naked corpse out to the street. Looking through the door she saw other corpses, some of them bloated and horrible – stinking. That image was imprinted clearly, deeply in her childhood mind, as was the fear and anger on her mother's face. Kate remembered nothing of her sisters and her brother dying.

But she had been told. Kate knew the reason why all this had happened – why hundreds, thousands like her father had been dumped naked into common graves and left to rot. "It is God's punishment of our sinful race," the priest had said. From that day her mother never smiled or laughed or loved. She showed no joy or sorrow in her dull dark eyes.

Kate could remember the bell at Saint Clement's Church tolling for the dead. For hours and hours the bell tolled. And then it was silent. Later she was told why. The man who pulled the bell rope had died.

"Move, Kate!" barked Maud, walking faster still. "My name is Katherine," the almost woman muttered, knowing well her mother couldn't hear, nor would she pay attention if she could. She could vaguely remember being Katherine as a child – a name she'd always loved and treasured, but which she hardly heard since that year of death.

Perhaps her mother had been softer then, before the dying – perhaps more tender. She wished her mother could forget, or at least forgive. But who? Forgive God perhaps? What were the sins that made God kill half the people of her town and send them without benefit of priest or mourners to an unconsecrated common grave? Why didn't her mother call her Katherine anymore?

There had hardly been a childhood for this almost woman. Her mother couldn't, wouldn't, care beyond the bare essentials for Thomas, who was born seven months after his father died. Kate found herself being mother to the boy. She cuddled him and fed him; she played with him and punished him, and took him into bed with her at night.

They were almost running now, around the corner onto Rouen Road, and there they slowed their pace. Here they passed the bakeshops, where the warm fulfilling smell of new baked bread pushed the pain away. Mother and daughter breathed more easily and Kate noticed that for just an instant her mother's face lightened a little. Perhaps it was the mounds of crisp, brown loaves fresh from the ovens that gave a wholesome sweetness to the fresh spring air, and just a touch of softness to her mother's face.

The towering hulk of the cathedral made it almost hard to notice the tiny church of Saint Julian silhouetted by the morning sun. Saint Julian's was unimposing, ordinary, like most of the sixty churches in Norwich. Who was this Saint Julian after whom the church was named, Kate wondered? Some said it was dedicated to Saint Julian the Hospitaller, the patron saint of those who sailed their tiny boats along the River Wensum just behind the church. Others claimed it was named after Bishop Julian of Le Mans, in France.

Saint Julian's was owned by the Benedictine Sisters at Carrow Abbey, who appointed the priests and derived the revenue from it. Made of small, dark flint stones stuck together with grey mortar, it looked so drab compared to the magnificence of the cathedral, which had been built with fine stone brought by sea from Caen, in Normandy, and floated on rafts up the Wensum.

"What a dreary little church," thought Kate, as her mother hurried her on without a glance. Down Hoborough Lane they went, toward her uncle's house – Uncle Robert, whom she remembered only vaguely, and not with pleasure. He never visited their family. Not since her father died, at least, leaving her widowed mother to care for an infant brother and Kate. Maud had asked for his help to manage their financial affairs. "I can't concentrate, Robert," she had said. "I need your help!"

Uncle Robert was heavy-set and sweating. Now that she saw him again, Kate remembered that he always seemed to sweat. "Come in, Maud. Kate. Sit there," he said. Kate wondered why they met inside, when just through the open door was a pleasant little courtyard where it was cool, and you could see the river, and Uncle Robert wouldn't sweat so much.

Uncle Robert had no time for small talk. "Meet Walter, son of Phillip Warren."

Maud didn't try to hide her look of disappointment. Uncle Robert blustered defensively, "Phillip is doing quite well and, ah, young Walter here has good prospects."

Kate glanced shyly at Walter, her husband to be. Young? Well, hardly. He was at least ten years her senior. Not very good looking, but strong and healthy at least. Not rich and tall and dashing as she had dreamed. But not small and old and ugly as she had feared. He was just so very ordinary.

Kate knew well enough that with her small dowry, and her

mother's modest circumstances, she had very little choice. When Walter rose to shake her hand, Kate recoiled slightly although she had resolved not to do that. It was that smell about him, the smell that triggered visions of the jaws of hell. But she touched his hand, then moved to stand beside her mother.

"Walter is following his father's trade. He's the only one left in his family, see! After the plague. So Walter gets to inherit Phillip's – that's his father – Walter gets the tanning shop when the time comes. That's if Phillip doesn't give it to the church to buy enough prayers to speed him out of purgatory. God knows they'll have a lot to pray about."

Walter blushed. Maud frowned. Kate felt a jolt of fear. "Enough chatter," said Uncle Robert. "So. Kate and Walter. The bans will be published at mass tomorrow by your priest in Saint Clement's Church and in the two weeks following. Four weeks from today – that's the wedding. You say your confession to the priest, and then get married at the church door. Phillip says there's a room above the tanning shop where you will live."

Uncle Robert stood. The conversation was over. Kate looked at Walter and forced a smile. Walter glanced at her, blushed, then looked intently at his hands. They were strong hands, noted Kate. Strong, but bruised and callused, dark as leather with dirt compacted under every fingernail.

Maud nodded a formal "Thank you," turned to leave, then stopped. "Robert. There's something else you should know. It's about Thomas. Kate's been looking after him because I don't have the stomach or the time for squalling children. He's too sickly for the wool trade. He might as well become a priest." Maud saw the painful surprise in Kate's face but paid no attention. "So I'm going to see the Prior at the Cathedral tomorrow."

There was no further conversation. Maud walked fast and angrily. Only as they hurried past the tanneries did her mother pause and point again to the nondescript shop.

"Mama!" Suddenly Kate was deeply fearful. "Mama! I don't know what to do. What do a husband and wife do when they get together? They get together naked, don't they?"

"Yes, naked," said Maud. "It's filthy and shameful and wicked, but God commands us to bear children, and that's the way you make babies. Then afterwards, we confess our sin."

"But what do I do, Mama, when we are together with each other?"

"You lie down on your back and you let him do whatever he wants. It will hurt at first. But it is necessary. It is a debt you pay for the honour of being his wife. You must do this whenever he wishes it. And after each time, you must confess your sin for doing it. Women inherit the sin of Eve."

Kate stopped. She tried to imagine herself living there – with the stink of hell around her, with Walter who seemed so ordinary. "Mother!" she called, then ran to catch up. "Will we learn to love each other?"

Her mother stopped. For a moment, it seemed to Kate, her face softened with a long forgotten memory, and then turned hard again. "It doesn't matter, Kate. You're no longer a child. You're a woman, and before the year is out you'll no doubt be screaming in the pain of childbirth. Pray to the Holy Virgin that God lets both you and the child live. Life is full of pain and sorrow. You'll get used to it, Kate."

They walked on in silence. "Yes," she thought. "I'll get used to being Kate." And the almost woman wept softly as they went.

—

She lay on her thin pallet of straw, waiting for the next shuddering spasm to run through her body, pushing down on the child within her. "That's right deary," said the midwife. "When you feel the pain a-comin' you push down. It's just like sittin' on the thunder bucket and havin' a good crap. Just push down hard. Say the *Ave Maria* girl! The Blessed Virgin will help you have a son."

Kate mumbled the *Ave Maria*. She knew it so well. She had said it and the *Pater Noster*, the Our Father, every day of her life since she learned to talk. She could say it even while her thoughts were elsewhere. And there was time to think now, between the contractions, to remember being married to Walter, there at the church door.

Walter had mumbled "with all my worldly goods I thee endow," and then muttered something of the endowment he pledged to Kate. He placed a brass ring and some money for the poor on the priest's book. Then Uncle Robert gave her away. The small group of friends and family that had gathered threw seeds at them and called, "Plenty! Plenty!" to wish them a large family. Uncle Robert had arranged a small bride-ale in the churchyard. A few cakes and sweets. Lots of ale.

Annora was there. She would enter the convent at Carrow in a few weeks – also a wedding of sorts – to become one of the "brides of Christ," as nuns were often called. The two young women hugged and wept for what had been and what was yet to be. Kate felt a pang of longing for the life Annora would lead in the convent, and Annora felt a twinge of jealousy that a husband had been found for Kate, but none for her.

Then Kate and Walter, her new father-in-law Phillip, Maud, Uncle Robert, and the priest walked to Walter's home. There the priest blessed the wedding bed to make it fertile.

Phillip kissed his new daughter-in-law and held her in his arms a bit longer than he should have, then gave each of his guests a cup of ale. They drank to the health of the bride and groom. Then they all went home.

So it was done. Walter had said nothing to Kate, except the few words the priest gave them to say at the church door when they were married. She didn't hear him speak to her until they came into the tiny room that was to be their home.

"I was married before, Kate." There was a tremor of embarrassment in his voice – or fear perhaps – as he blurted out what sounded like confession. "I was married once before, but she died with the first baby."

Kate instinctively needed to respond to the pain and confusion she saw in her new husband's eyes. She wanted to take his hand and hold him. For the first time, she felt something that might have been affection for this muscled, fearful male.

Suddenly, Walter began to remove his clothes, but in his movements Kate sensed more dread than desire. He motioned to her to do likewise. She obeyed. Her mother had given her several lectures since the day of her betrothal. "You must obey your husband in all things," said Maud. "Holy Church teaches that the man is the head of the household. He is the strong one. A woman is the weaker vessel. She must do as she is bidden."

Kate had imagined she would be embarrassed to have a man look on her nakedness. But she was conscious more of Walter's trembling hands. She lay down on the bed, and Walter lay down beside her. For a long time they just lay there, staring at the thatched roof above them. No words. Then on impulse, Kate took Walter's callused hand.

And Walter began to cry.

Kate had never seen a grown man cry, but it seemed right that he should do so. He cried deep primeval sobs that shuddered through his body, tears that came from who knows where in the childhood that he never had – tears a man was not supposed to shed.

And then another impulse. Kate took this strange man, her husband now, gently in her arms and held him closely, just as she had held Thomas, her baby brother, when he cried for the mother Maud could never be to him. She held Walter close to her, and then slowly she felt his arms embracing her. And so it was with infant love their vows were sealed. Silently Kate breathed a prayer of thanks.

Kate's reverie was interrupted by another contraction, this one stronger than before. "Keep pushin' sweetheart," urged the midwife. "It won't be long. And keep sayin' them *Aves*, Kate! You've got to keep sayin' them or the babe will die inside you."

"It hurts so much," wailed Kate. "It hurts!"

"Of course it hurts. It's the punishment God sends to all us womenfolk because Eve took the apple from the snake and started sin. There's nothin' to be done for it. Push hard and keep saying them *Aves*."

So Kate said the *Aves* as commanded, though as the contraction subsided, her thoughts turned to Walter again. He was not a man of many words. But he was a good man, Kate soon learned. Good and gentle. In their short and tired times together at night before they slept, she and Walter talked a little. And sometimes they made love and Kate would think herself to sleep wondering how such gentle joy could be a sin.

She wished there was more time to talk. To rest together. To think. Each day, from sunup to sundown, she worked wordlessly beside Walter in the tanner's shop, her eyes streaming from the smell of it. Kate mostly worked at scraping hides, removing any remaining bits of fat or flesh. Phillip kept for himself the important work of buying hides from the butchers – the hides of cows, sheep, and pigs. And he supervised the two apprentices, who scurried around doing the jobs that he didn't want to do.

Walter had to do the work the apprentices could not be trusted with, especially anything involving money. That's why Walter had the task of gathering the supplies needed to tan the hides – he brought into the shop the urine and feces people would collect in their chamber pots. Dog dung was better for tanning than human waste, however, and Walter would patrol the streets collecting whatever he could find, usually before light each morning, before the other tanners had picked the streets clean. Walter and the other tanners called dog dung, "pure." Pure gave leather a deep rich brown color, much deeper than inferior human waste.

Walter never said it, but Kate knew he found the work degrading and often humiliating, especially when people made bad jokes at his expense.

Still, he sometimes had the grace to make jokes about himself. "It's a wonderful high callin'. I keep the whole neighbourhood smelling sweet and clean. I bring all the stink home with me." And sometimes he showed unexpected compassion. "I had two of 'em tried to do it to me." Walter shook his head sadly. "They shape their own shit by stretching it out long and thin, like. And they put dust on it to make it look like a dog's dropping."

"What did you do?" Kate had asked.

"I didn't do nothin'," he shrugged. "Can you imagine folks being so hard up they have to handle their own shit just to get an extra farthing outa me? So I paid 'em."

Pelts were soaked in urine to loosen the hair so it could be scraped off with the sharp edge of a scudder. This rawhide was then placed for "bating" in a nauseating brew of dog and human dung, to fluff open the pores of the hide and make it soft and pliant and turn it tawny brown. To determine the strength of the bath, Walter used the time-honoured test. He put his finger in the bubbling brew and tasted it.

The final process involved the bark of trees, usually oak, which was soaked in water to extract tannin. The hides were soaked in a series of baths, each one with more tannin in it.

Each night as soon as darkness began to fall, Walter, Kate, Phillip, and the two apprentices, who slept between the stinking vats in the tannery, shared a quick, bland meal of bread, fish, and ale. Walter's father did all the talking, prattling endlessly about the cost of hides from the butchers down the street, complaining about the neighbours, wondering if there was a widow somewhere he could lure into his bed. Each night, before she climbed the ladder to their room, Kate would dutifully kiss the beads of sweat on his long forehead, and he would pat her buttocks in a way that suggested more than fatherly affection.

Kate often wondered if she loved Walter and if Walter loved her. Yes, there were times of tenderness and affection. But was that love? Love was hardly spoken of among the trading folk and crafters in the neighbourhood. Romantic love was hardly necessary in the marriage bed. Marriage was a contract – an agreement between two families hoping to build social and financial strength from the arrangement.

Romance was for young girls like Kate and Annora to dream about, and for the rich and gallant knights who sang sweet songs to noble ladies. Not to their own wives, of course, but to women who were married to some noble lord. Love was a dream, a game for those who could afford it – a recreation for the knights and ladies. Courtly love was there to fill the times between the wars, which were the noble knight's true occupation.

Those like Kate and Walter, who worked and struggled for their bread, could hope for neither love nor romance. They lived on prayer, blind luck, hard, hard work, and grim fatalism. "You take what you get," Walter shrugged. "You do the best you can for as long as you live and hope that when you die God will be kind to you and not punish you too hard."

Exhausted, Kate and Walter fell into bed each night. Sometimes there was sex. Sometimes Kate began to feel some love in the sex. And sometimes there was conversation, lying on the mouldy, straw-filled mattress, trying to avoid the bed bugs, waiting for sleep.

Often she and Walter talked of small things – the price the butchers asked for raw hides, the biting winds that blew down from the North Sea in winter, the ugly smell of tanning Kate hardly noticed anymore – but in those small conversations, she sensed a growing warmth. Walter was a decent man, a kind man, even if he hardly knew how to speak of such things.

He didn't get that from his father, Kate thought. Phillip swore and yelled and threw leering glances at her. When she complained to Walter about his father's roving hands he had nothing more than a helpless shrug to offer. "He's been like that since mother died,"

"How did she die?" Kate asked.

"The pestilence," Walter muttered woodenly. "Her and my two brothers. Papa's been acting strange ever since. Always trying to seduce any woman nearby. I think he's mad at God."

"My mother is too. And well she should be!" Kate surprised herself with her own vehemence. Was she also angry at God?

"It's a sin to be angry at God," blurted Walter. "That's what priests say. Your mother and my father will scream in hell if they're angry at God."

Another sharp contraction left Kate gasping for air. The contractions were coming more quickly now. "That's right, deary!" coaxed the midwife. "Just keep pushing down. We'll have that baby out in no time."

As Kate's belly blossomed, Walter seemed to show a touch of tenderness to her sometimes. "Go sit awhile," he would say. Kate would straighten her aching back and lie on a wooden bench in a room beside the tannery. The ladder to their room upstairs was so hard for her to climb now, she didn't want to do it more than once a day.

She often gazed at a coarsely bound book on an alcove shelf nearby. Kate wondered why she was so fascinated. "You keep your hands off that, woman!" Phillip had said when he caught her looking at it. "It's a valuable piece of property and I don't want you messing with it. Four shillings! That's what I paid for it. You can't read it anyway."

That was true. Nor could Phillip for that matter, although sometimes he took down the book and turned the leaves. For him it was an investment, which he would sell when the price and time was right.

Kate thought she could read a few words of Latin. For just one season, because there was no money for any more than that, Maud had sent Kate to live with the nuns at Carrow. They taught her some words of Latin – how to read some of the prayers and psalms from their missal. Perhaps "read" wasn't the right word. Mostly the girls memorized the psalms, though sometimes the nuns told them which marks on the paper stood for which words. Kate wanted to learn more but the teaching sister shook her head. "That's all a woman needs to know. Just enough to say your prayers."

"*Benedicte Domine!*" Kate hissed through clenched teeth, as a shudder and a contraction greater than all the others rumbled through her body.

"The baby's coming," squealed the midwife. "Right way round too, by the looks of it. Push hard, Kate! It's your first child, and you're not big. Push hard now. There's a dear!"

And then the pain overwhelmed her. Kate had never known anything that hurt so much; it was more than she could bear. The room became dark and she saw herself and Annora standing in the cathedral close, watching the mystery plays – watching Christ retch out his life on a cross and she could smell the blood and the pain which was just too terrible to bear, and she heard Jesus scream, "My God!

My God! Why have you abandoned me?" and the voice came from the figure on the cross but the voice was her own voice and the pain was her own pain, and then, with one great tearing heave, it was done. Kate was a mother.

"Aw, it's a girl," said the disappointed midwife. "Keep trying deary. You'll have a boy next time. Wear a sprig of rosemary around your neck when your man's gettin' into ya. That'll make it a boy for sure."

Then the midwife washed the babe in a tub of warm water. She gently rubbed the tiny fingers and toes. "That chases the evil humours out," she explained. Next she dipped her finger in honey and used it to clean the baby's palate and gums. "Do ya have some wine anywhere?" she asked Kate.

Kate shook her head weakly. "Just some ale in the jug in the next room."

"That'll do, I suppose. Wine's better." The midwife took a mouthful of ale and forced it into the infant's mouth. "Help's her suck better."

"You're a papa now," the midwife said to Walter when she called him in. And Kate's heart swelled in love and hope and gratitude as Walter cradled his tiny, soft, white, newborn daughter in his big, dark, callused hands.

"What shall we call her?" Walter's voice had a gentleness Kate had not heard before. "I'd like to call her Katherine, but I think we have to name her Maud or your mother will be angry."

—

Mothering came easily to Kate. She had been a mother to her baby brother Thomas when she was barely seven winters old. "Take care of him," Maud had barked. Kate did the best she could, and gradually learned the art.

Kate treasured the quiet moments when she nursed baby Maud. Especially in the middle of the night, when all the noises of the street and shop were stilled, when she woke in the velvet darkness to the tiny cry of little Maud beside her in bed. These were times of meditation, of holiness for Kate, as she held the infant to her breast and felt her life flow into this helpless newborn soul. Kate wasn't sure if it was prayer or not, but her reverie sometimes brought a sense of closeness, of a holy presence, and many times she thought God's nurturing love must be like the mothering love she felt as she fed the child with herself. In those moments she could not imagine anger at the tiny, helpless infant in her arms, or imagine how a God who created such a wondrous child could feel anger toward it.

And yet, in the clear light of day, she remembered the teaching of the priests and the nuns at Carrow, of a God of wrath and anger, of a God who punished sin and sent the refining fire of pain and death to wayward children. Then she knew her midnight reveries were pleasant fantasies. Nothing more.

Kate had sent word to her mother when the time of her delivery was near, hoping Maud would come and be with her. But there was no response. Kate had not really expected any.

It was two weeks before Kate had the strength to undertake the half-hour walk to her mother's house. "I'm taking the baby to see her grandmother," she said to Walter. "I want her to bless my child, even if she can't love it."

The soft stink of wet wool greeted Kate as she walked into the house that held a lifetime of bittersweet memories. Maud, hunched over a bale of wool she was tying, did not look up. She was sorting – packing wool that had been spun by a dozen women in their homes and was readying it to be shipped to weavers across the Channel in Flanders. Nearby, an apprentice washed a tub of wool, picking burrs and bits of wood and grass from the mass of fibre.

Maud was running the wool business on her own now. Two months after the first wave of pestilence had ended, her jaw set in grim determination, Maud found the house where lived the master of the Wool Merchant's Guild. There she declared herself *femme sole*, the owner, operator of the business left by her dead husband. She did the necessary things, and the business, while it didn't prosper, didn't completely fail either. But her heart was never in it.

Maud had a hard time finding people to work for her. There was just one helper left of the four who once did the washing and the packing, and that was Uncle Robert's awkward nephew. Two had died in the plague, and the other had left to work for higher wages. Plague had hit the working classes and the serfs far more severely than the mercantile or noble class, who were healthier and stronger simply because they had enough to eat.

Maud could find no one else to work for her – no one to apprentice in the trade. Nor did she have much will to search for help. Where once there had been thirty women spinning wool for her in their houses, now she had only a dozen. Her shop sat half empty. The wool trade gave Maud just enough income to survive.

"Mother!" Kate said. "I've come to show you your grandchild."

"If he lives to be seven or eight years old, that's time enough to get to know him. Then if he can pack or wash wool he'll be of use to us. Most babies die before they walk, you know." Maud plunked herself angrily onto a chair near the window.

"I know that, Mother." Kate spoke softly, passionately. "That's why I've come for your blessing. It's a girl. I want you to bless your granddaughter. Her name is Maud."

Kate saw it. For just a moment, there was mist in her mother's eyes. Her lip trembled. Then she found control again. "Don't bother me with that nonsense. I have work to do."

"Mama," said Kate, this time in tears. "Mama! Listen! You are going to bless your granddaughter whether you want to or not." The baby wailed and Kate, with anger and despair, placed the crying infant firmly in her grandmother's lap. The child sobbed louder, as Maud stared with set jaw at the blankness of a wall. But Kate could see the lip that trembled. Kate could see the lines of grim avoidance slowly melting.

"Here. Take this squalling brat!" Maud's voice cracked and trembled.

"She is your grandchild!" shouted Kate, desperation shaking her words. The apprentice dropped his soggy wool and scurried out the door. "She is your grandchild, Mama! Bless her! Please bless her, Mama!"

"I have no blessings left, Kate. I died that day your brother and your sisters and your father died. Can't you see it, Kate? I'm a walking corpse. You have no mother. This baby has no grandmother. Everything is dead. I have cursed God to His face, and now I live in hell. Don't you understand that, Kate?"

"Mama. Please, just look at the baby. Just look at her. Just once, please Mama!"

Tiny Maud stopped crying, though infant teardrops lingered in her eyes, looking up toward her grandmother. Finally, in spite of herself, Maud looked. She looked, and slowly her face began to soften. Kate said nothing, though she sensed the beginning of a miracle.

Then old Maud lifted baby Maud gently to her face. Pent-up tears streamed freely from her eyes. Kate knelt beside her mother, one arm cradling her shoulder, the other cradling her baby. Once again the child began to wail.

Then all three of them cried. It was such wonder of a wailing, such a joyous sobbing and a mopping up of tears, with bits of laughter too.

Years later, Kate would remember this moment and know that God was present with them in their miracle – crying, laughing, with them.

1359

And I felt the sadness
and then the joy,
first one and then the other – many times.
This vision showed me
it is necessary for some souls to feel this way –
sometimes to be in comfort
and sometimes to fail and to be left by themselves.
But sin is not always the cause.
Freely, God gives us what we need,
and sometimes lets us suffer pain.
Both are part of one love.

I can't make it work anymore," she said to Robert. "Ever since the pestilence, it..." Her shoulders slumped. "I can't do it! Nobody will work for me unless I pay them a king's ransom. The only one who has stayed on is that half-witted nephew of yours. And I can't find enough women to spin for me."

"It's everywhere, Maud," said her brother-in-law. "The villeins don't know their place anymore. They haggle over wages as if they were free men, and the lords pay them more. They go from one lord to the other as if they had a right to leave the land they were born on and just go wherever there's more money. It's the fault of the lords. Sure it is! They rob each other. They seduce the serfs with promises. Villeins no longer know their station. The times are troubled." They shook their heads in sad agreement.

"The villeins are acting as if they are free men!" Maud's voice rose in indignation. "And the apprentices are worse. The only good one I had left just walked out one day. No 'by-your-leave' – as if he was at liberty to go where he wanted. Just like that!"

"I am *femme sole* in my spinning craft." Maud sat down heavily on the stool Robert offered. "For all these years since my husband and children coughed out their lives in the pestilence, I've been trapped in that shop, in that house, in that craft. I've been trapped in my own anger. But Kate brought me her baby for its grandmother's kiss. And now I have no stomach left for the smell of wet wool. I don't want to tear my aching knuckles packing bales any longer. I have a plan, Robert."

"And so have I, Maud," Robert interjected. "You've scorned every man that has come to you. You've been a widow for more than ten years, Maud. I have heard tell how you used a stick to drive away your suitors..."

"They wanted nothing but my money and my..."

"Of course. What else would they want? Why else would they marry and give their name and their bed to a woman?"

"I have a plan, Robert. Listen..."

"You listen to me, woman! You are my dead brother's wife and you owe me some respect and fealty..."

"And you have been a widower that same long time, Robert. Where is your new wife?"

"Maud! Maud! God's bones, woman! It does us no good to quarrel. I will marry you. I will give you my bed and my name and I will take over your business. You will be secure in your old age, and I will be comforted."

Maud stood up, her eyes blazing. "You're an old fool, Robert!"

"Of course I'm an old fool!" The sweat was running down his forehead. "So are you! Listen to some sense..."

"You can have my business, Robert. Or at least most of it. I have no use for your bed or your name. I want neither. I have no great needs – just food and shelter. You can buy that for me at Carrow Abbey. I want to stay there so I can live in safety and so I can walk over to Kate's place any time to watch my grandchild grow."

Robert snorted. "And how do you plan to manage that?"

"I will give you my house, my craft, and all that I own except my own clothes and a few keepsakes. You can sell it or keep the business for yourself. You will buy a corrody for me at Carrow Abbey so that I can live there till I die. A corrody will ensure that the nuns give me food, clothing, and a place to live for the rest of my life. What more do I need? If I learn to pray again, I will pray for the peace of your soul as I will pray for my husband and my children. And my newborn granddaughter."

"Why not simply take the veil and be done with it," Robert sniffed. "If you plan to pray your life away in that cloister, why not become a nun?"

"Don't be ridiculous. I have no such vocation, Robert. My knees are sore enough in winter, I don't plan to hurt them more by kneeling to pray the hours seven times each day, especially not in the middle of the cold winter nights. A corrody will do just fine, and cost you less than the dowry to become a nun."

—

Maud was there with Kate when the second child was born. "No," she had said to Kate. "I don't want to be your midwife. You need someone who knows what to do if things go wrong. I will hold your hand and help you through."

Maud simply moved in when Kate's time was near. Walter protested just a little, and his father quite a bit. "Am I to pay for all her food?" Phillip demanded. But Maud waved them both away and told Walter to go sleep in the room with his father, even though Walter took her aside and tried to explain that his father snored dreadfully.

"Then sleep downstairs in the tannery," she said.

Kate's second child came easily, just as the midwife had predicted, and they dutifully named the new boy baby Phillip after his randy grandfather. Walter greeted his new son with the same strong tenderness he had for his daughter. This amazed and delighted Kate. Men were not expected to show such care and gentleness to children. Their duty was to discipline the children – to cane them thoroughly, to scold and admonish.

But Walter was a different kind of father, though he denied it strongly whenever his own father would comment on it. Walter hardly raised his voice to his children. He rejoiced in every small accomplishment and kissed away every tear.

He was a different kind of husband, too. Tears of joy filled Kate's eyes the day he first called her Katherine. "How did you know?" she asked. Walter smiled, shrugged his shoulders, and went back to his work.

And Maud was better than her word. She came to see her grandchildren and her daughter every week, though she never failed to complain about the smell of the tannery. "How do you breath around here?" she asked every time. Sometimes she knit clothes or did mending for them. And sometimes on a Sunday, Kate would take the children to visit Maud at the abbey. There the air was pure and the children could find grass to crawl or run on.

Carrow Abbey was poorer by far than the monastery attached to Norwich Cathedral. King Stephen endowed his many male monastic foundations with far more money than he gave to Carrow, but even so it was the wealthiest female convent in Norfolk County.

Carrow had been given good land and the villeins that were considered part of that land. That, and the income from Saint Julian's Church, made the abbey quite self-sufficient. The abbess, often to the annoyance of her bishop, was remarkably independent of the power structures in the city. She held court for her bond and free tenants. She proved wills. The convent even maintained a gallows – a lucrative privilege because the crowds that came to witness every hanging could be sold food and drink and trinkets.

Most of the female convents in Norfolk were far from towns

and cities. Wisdom had it that women needed isolation and poverty – freedom from temptation – to make them acceptable "brides of Christ." But Carrow was near the South Gate of Norwich. It was a major influence on the spiritual lives of women in the city.

Like most monasteries in England, Carrow was dominated by the abbey church, which (like most churches) also faced east toward Jerusalem. South of the church, sheltered from the cold North Sea winds, was the cloister, which the nuns had nicknamed "Paradise." Here the women could walk in the few short moments of leisure they had in their busy work-filled, prayer-punctuated days and nights.

Opening onto the cloister were the chapter house where meetings were held, and the refectory where meals were taken. Nearby was the abbess' apartment, on top of which was the small library – the only building in the convent that was heated in the cold winter. Also nearby were the infirmary, and the *necessarium.*

A large garden was tended by Sister Joan. Joan was Kate's girlhood friend Annora Parke, who had taken her vows and her new name-in-religion soon after Kate's wedding. She was also the herbalist in the convent. Her garden was full of plants used for healing. She grew vegetables and herbs for flavouring food. The garden was separated from the convent by the huts of the corrodians.

Maud chose to live as a corrodian at Carrow, because it was one of the few ways an unattached woman could live in relative peace. Maud was an exception, of course. For most women, there were only three career options: marriage, the convent, or prostitution. Both marriage and the convent usually required a dowry.

The nuns at Carrow were confined. Only the abbess was permitted to leave the grounds. But Carrow was not an insulated community. There were twenty-seven nuns at Carrow when Maud walked through the gates, but there were also two priests and twenty-eight boarders and corrodians.

From the abbey kitchen, Maud received a daily allowance of food; two white loaves of bread, assorted other foods, and a large jug of ale. The convent also provided her with 200 faggots or sticks,

100 logs a year for fuel, and eight pounds of candles. In addition, there would be a new set of clothes each year for her and her maid, and the care and ministrations of the nuns and the resident clergy if she became ill.

For this Uncle Robert paid an "outrageous" sum of twenty pounds. "They should treat you like a duchess for that kind of money!" he spluttered. But Robert knew and Maud knew that her lot was little better than the frugal life the nuns lived. She had a small hut to herself though, a hut with two rooms. One for herself, and one for a maid. If she had a maid. There was little in the way of furniture. In each room a chair, a small table, a straw mattress on the dirt floor, and a ring of stones in the middle for a fire and a hole in the roof for the smoke to escape.

"Sometimes we have women come to us," said Mother Cecily, the abbess. "Women who need a place in life. Such a one might become a maid to you. But for now, you'll have to manage on your own."

"I'm not sure I need or want a maid," Maud said to Mother Cecily. "It's a tiny hut and my food will come from the refectory. I'll need to move my bones about a little with a bit of housework." The abbess shrugged and walked back to the chapter house.

It was a good, rich time for Maud, perhaps the best three years of her life. Freed from the daily grind of the wool trade, Maud found herself at loose ends at first. She surprised herself by attending six of the seven times of worship, mandatory for the nuns, but optional to her. "Well," said Maud, "I don't rouse myself for the night office, but I've been pretty good about going to all the others. Some of those poor women fall asleep on their knees, they're so tired." Although she understood very little of the Latin liturgy, Maud found the rhythm of worship deeply nourishing and the singing of the nuns washed her wounded soul in ways she had not expected.

But she did not pray. She could not pray. She refused to pray. The anger, the depression, returned in waves sometimes, as she sat the hours away in her little hut. She never talked to any of the nuns about it.

She did talk to Kate, though. When days passed and Maud stayed alone in her small hut nursing the darkness in her soul, Kate sometimes bundled up her babies and came looking for her. "I still cannot pray, Kate," she explained. "God wouldn't listen to my prayers. I cursed God when your father and sisters and brother died. I told God I hated him. I told God I'd given my soul to Satan, because Satan, at least, doesn't pretend to love us while he destroys us."

"Do you still hate God?"

"Not always. Sometimes. Until you came in the door with little Maud and placed her screaming in my lap, I hated God. When I sit here in the dark, I still hate God."

"I don't think God killed our family," said Kate. "I don't think God sent the pestilence to kill half the people of Norwich. We are God's children. The priest tells us that. The priests say God loves us. So why? How? How could God kill his children? You know, Mother, sometimes, in the middle of the night, little Phillip wakes me with his hunger." Maud smiled. She remembered those times. "I hold him close to me and give him my breast. It seems such a holy and beautiful time and I think – it seems God must love us the way I love my babies."

Maud had no answer. But she found tears to shed and then Kate gave her the smallest child to hold. "Mother," she said. "Look after the children for a while. I'll be back very soon."

Maud looked puzzled but offered no objection. Kate walked over to the abbey to find Sister Joan. She and Kate found it easy to renew their friendship when Maud moved to Carrow – to remember the fantasies of their childhood. But this time Kate was concerned about her mother, and Sister Joan was the healer in the convent. She understood the work of herbs and potions, and sometimes brought relief and hope to ailing nuns and other residents at Carrow.

"Here," said Sister Joan. "Brew these dry leaves in boiling water. Make it strong. Tell your mother to drink a good cup of brew just before she joins us for prayers."

"What is it?"

"It's called Saint John's Wort. It blooms bright yellow in the spring on the feast day of Saint John the Baptist. It's good for lots of things. For complaints of the stomach, for sleeplessness – and when the humours of the body are unbalanced. Your mother is suffering from melancholia, and this brew will help."

"Thank you, Sister Joan."

"But Kate, why is your mother still so angry at God?"

Kate looked up startled. "Did she tell you that?"

"No. But I see it in her face. I see it when she comes to hear the hours sung. Is she still angry that your family died in the pestilence?"

"Mother has never forgiven God."

Now it was Sister Joan's turn to be startled. "She would forgive God?"

Kate stood and walked toward the door, then turned back. "The priest in our parish said that the deathly plague was God's punishment for our sins. He said that God could no longer tolerate our evil, sinful race and was destroying everything, as in Noah's time. Mother wants to know – and yes, *I* want to know too – what sins could bring such penalty."

"Do you believe God sent the pestilence, Kate?" Joan asked thoughtfully.

Kate took time to think before she answered. "No."

"Neither do I. I don't know why we suffered such horror. I don't know why our lives are full of pain and death. And ugliness." Sister Joan closed her eyes tightly. She spoke very softly. "I don't know, Kate. And sometimes I feel the darkness in my soul. You know I wanted marriage, not the convent. But there was no knight riding on a white horse. My father couldn't find a good, profitable match, so here I am in the convent."

"Are you angry, Joan?" Kate was almost afraid to ask the question.

"Yes. Sometimes I wake up in the darkness, full of anger. But when I cry out, I see the cross, Kate. I see God on the cross – bleeding, suffering, and dying. I don't know why we must suffer, but I know that God suffers with us. In spite of what the bishop may say."

Kate took the small bag of dried leaves from her friend and heated water in the small kettle that hung over her mother's fire pit. She watched the smoke curl through the hole in the roof and when the kettle boiled she offered her mother the dark brown brew. "It does taste rather vile," Maud shuddered after gagging on the first sip. "I suppose that means it's good for me."

"You're to drink this before you go to hear the hours sung, Mother. Seven times a day."

"Why just before the hours? As it is, I sometimes have to run to the *necessarium* to pee before the singing's done."

"Just try it, Mother. Sister Joan says it will help you through your melancholia, through the blackness in your soul." Maud still looked skeptical.

"And Sister also says she doesn't think God sent the pestilence. She says to look at the crucifix, because there you see God suffering with us. God knows the pain we feel."

It was no instant cure – neither the brew nor the preachments. But one day Maud heard herself humming an old folk song to her grandchildren. She hadn't heard herself sing in years.

Lollay, Lollay, little child,
Why do you weep so, my child?
You weep because you know, my child,
It is your destiny, to live in misery.
Lollay, Lollay, my child.

"What a dreadful song," Maud thought to herself. She tried to remember when she had learned it. "On the other hand," she sighed, "it's probably the truth. It's probably the truth."

—

The autumn leaves were swirling through the grass that morning when Kate and her babies came for their usual Sunday visit with Maud. But this time Maud wasn't in her hut. Kate found her kneeling in the chapel, praying. "I am praying for my grandchildren," she said.

"Have you forgiven God?"

"God doesn't need to be forgiven." She reached out and took little Phillip from Kate. "Sister Joan said God hears all the prayers we make, even if we ourselves are in a state of sin. I've tried, but I still can't pray for the souls of your father and your dead brother and sisters. But I have been able to pray for you and for the babies."

"What about yourself? Have you...?"

"No, Katherine. I have not been able to pray for myself."

"Oh, Mother!" Tears welled up in Kate's eyes.

"What have I said?"

"You called me Katherine! You haven't called me Katherine since before the pestilence, and that is the name I have always cherished."

Maud looked down in sadness. Then she took her daughter's hand. "I have been cruel to you, haven't I? All those years I was so despondent, so angry. You had to take care of poor little Thomas all by yourself. And I called you Kate even though I knew you hated it. I'll never call you that again."

Katherine smiled and put her arm gently around her mother's shoulder. Maud put her arm around her daughter's waist and took the hand of little Maud, now a toddler. Together, they walked from the chapel to the hut where Maud lived. No words were needed. It was simply good to feel the love they shared. "Leave the babies here with me," Maud pleaded. "It's a lovely day and I can watch them play on the grass. I'll bring them to you before nightfall."

As she neared her home, Katherine smelled the tannery but suppressed the gorge that rose in her throat – the image of death which the stink so often brought to mind. Instead, she smiled. Her life was not what she had fantasized. She was neither a virgin saint nor a noble lady. Her gallant knight was a stocky, inarticulate tanner, who was kind, gentle, and loving in his own awkward way. Nor did she envy the closely ordered life she saw her virginal sisters live at Carrow Abbey. She breathed a prayer of thanks for her mother's continuing recovery, threw her shoulders back against the smell of death, and opened the door into the tanner's shop.

Phillip was there. Alone. Katherine felt a tightness in her throat.

She had no love for her father-in-law. "He's an old bull's pizzle," she steamed one day at Walter, after Phillip's roving hands had made her day a nightmare.

Katherine had been mentally preparing for this day. Phillip grinned his lechery across the room at her. He wiped his dung-stained hands against his dirty apron as he walked toward her. She stood her ground and looked him in the eye.

"Listen old man," she hissed. "I know exactly what you have in mind. If you lay one hand on me, I'll smash your knackers so you can't stand up for a week. And I'll tell everybody in town the reason why."

Phillip stopped. He face turned beet red. His chest heaved. His eyes glistened with confusion and fear. He turned and walked back to the vat where he'd been working. And Katherine wondered if she'd won the war. Or was it just this skirmish?

It was the war. Phillip's face was often red, Katherine noted. Whenever he exerted himself a little, whenever he was irritated, which was often, whenever he drank more ale than he should, which too was often, his face turned florid. Katherine knew it was unhealthy and that often such people died suddenly.

Phillip collapsed a month later, getting up from his bed in the morning. Katherine took her babies to their grandmother and nursed her father-in-law for three days and nights, wiping his face and praying gently at his side. On the fourth day, he was lucid for a while. He sent Walter to get the priest. "I need to make my peace with God."

Katherine sat down beside her father-in-law, his face now contorted and flushed, as if struggling with some inner demon. Several times he took a breath, as if to speak. "Try to rest," she said as she wiped his beaded forehead. "God is merciful. You have nothing to fear."

"I have..." He paused to swallow. "Kate – I tried...will you forgive me?"

"Yes, of course," she said. There was no need to name the sin. Then she leaned over and kissed him on the forehead, surprised at the affection she felt for this lonely, dying man.

"The book," Phillip said. Speaking was hard for him now. "The book in the room downstairs. Yours. You…you are clever, Kate. You can learn. I could make no sense of it."

When the priest came in, he motioned Walter and Katherine to leave the room. "I must hear your father's confession. When he is shriven, you may come back into the room and pray with us."

It seemed to Katherine to have been a very short confession when the priest called them back into Phillip's room. He began his Latin prayers: "Remember not, oh Lord, our iniquities, nor the iniquities of our forefathers. Spare us, good Lord, spare thy people, whom thou hast redeemed with thy most precious blood, and be not angry with us forever. *Kyrie eleison* – Lord have mercy upon us."

"*Christe eleison* – Christ have mercy upon us," replied Walter and Katherine automatically.

"*Kyrie eleison*," continued the priest. His Latin prayers seemed to drone on forever. Then he anointed Phillip with holy oil and made the sign of the cross once again. The priest took the crucifix which hung on the wall over Phillip's bed and put it in the dying man's hands. "Keep your eyes on this cross as you die, my son," he said, "so that the devil may not claim your soul." Then he made the sign of the cross toward Walter and Katherine, and left.

Phillip, who'd had his eyes closed the whole time the priest was there, looked at them and tried to smile. "Walter," he said in a whisper. "Come close. I have some words to say to you." Walter knelt by his bed. "Walter, the book. For Kate. I want her to have it. I didn't…" he coughed violently and Katherine urged him to rest. "I treated her badly. She's very clever…maybe she can read…and pay the priests…prayers…for my soul. Not too many…I don't want you… not too many prayers. A few."

Katherine and Walter took turns throughout the night, sitting beside him, holding his hand, holding up the cross for him whenever his eyes opened. And in the morning, Phillip died peacefully with Katherine holding his hand. She gently closed his eyes and went to put her arms around her husband. Walter needed to cry; Katherine could see that. But she would never suggest such a thing to her husband. So she stood and held him for as long as he would let her. "I must go to the priest and arrange the burial," said Walter, his voice croaking as he spoke. He pulled away and left.

Katherine made her way down the ladder into the small room where the book rested on the tiny shelf. She'd never held a book before, much less owned one. And this was hers! She opened it and looked slowly at the pages. The rows of tiny marks made no sense to her, though she tried as best she could to remember her scant learning from the short time she had at Carrow, where she had been taught to read some phrases from the Latin prayer book. But she held the book tightly nonetheless, and wondered if it would someday yield its secret to her.

1362

In this love without beginning God made us,
and protects us
and never allows us to receive harm.
And so when the judgment is given
and we are all brought to heaven,
then we shall clearly see in God
the secrets which are now hidden from us.
Then none of us will want to say,
"Lord, if it had been this way or that,
then all things would have been well."
But we will say with one voice:
"Lord, may you be blessed!
because, indeed, all is well."

Walter came back from his morning gathering dung and urine. He looked pale and shaken. "The cathedral steeple has been toppled, Katherine. They say it crashed last night in the storm. They say it is an omen. A bad omen. God is angry with our city and God will punish us!"

"But what have we done?" Katherine held little Phillip closer. "What are we being punished for?"

Walter gently ran his rough hand over the soft, smooth skin of his tiny son, shook his head, and shrugged. Katherine could see the fear in his eyes, the fear she felt in her heart, the nameless fear of a God who sets impossible, secret standards, and then exacts terrible punishment when humans fail. Walter went down the ladder to the tannery and began to scrub a cowhide. He scrubbed until the sweat beaded on his forehead, until the work brought some relief from fear. Katherine nursed her year-old child and prayed, "Holy Mother, intercede for us. Holy Mother, save us. Holy Mother, you know what it is like to fear for your child. Holy Mother, what have we done? Why is God angry?"

—

The question was not answered. The crime was never named. But the penalty came soon and hard. "The pestilence is back!" Walter yelled as he ran in the door. "Katherine! The pestilence is come again! Don't go outside! Close the shutters and bolt the door! Do you hear me, Katherine?"

Yes, she heard him. But it didn't matter. Katherine was cradling, rocking little Phillip. It began with small red rashes in his armpits and groin. They quickly swelled to red-hot boils and the baby screamed in pain. As the hideous buboes grew, little Phillip lost the strength to cry. He seemed to be asleep behind his dull, unseeing eyes. Katherine didn't need to hear Walter's dreadful news. Her baby was dying in her arms.

Walter carried the tiny body through the cold, dark, drizzling rain to Saint Julian's Church to have it blessed and buried. Katherine did not go because she feared now for her second child, little Maud, just three years old, just discovering her world. Her fear was realized two days later. Little Maud, like her brother Phillip, died in Katherine's arms.

Once again, Walter, his eyes flaming, his face contorted in fearful pain and anger, stumbled through the drizzling rain to the church, this time with the body of his second child. He did not return.

Katherine knew, somehow, that he wouldn't. Though Walter might be wandering the streets somewhere, he had died with his two children, just as she had died. Life, it seemed, was over for them.

Katherine waited in her empty home – waited for...what? Rocking back and forth, back and forth. Not weeping. Not moving. Not eating. Not sleeping. Rocking. For two days she rocked and waited. Then, with clenched teeth and shallow breath, she picked up her extra clothes and walked towards the door into the rain. She stopped, turned, and went back to get her book, the book that Phillip gave her, though she wondered why. Then she stumbled down the muddy road to Carrow Abbey. She had nowhere else to go.

The exhausted priest found Katherine in her mother's hut. "They found your husband's body in the Wensum," he said bluntly. "Did he kill himself or did he fall?"

Katherine looked at the priest and then at Maud. Dry eyed, unblinking, she found the strength to say it. "He must have fallen." As she said it, Katherine knew how deeply she had loved this quiet, fearful man, and so she told the loving lie. If Walter's death was suicide, he could not be buried by the priest in consecrated ground.

But the lie was not a lie, when all was said and done. It was the plague, it was God who killed her husband. She shuddered, knowing she had just accused God of murder. Who killed her babies? Who killed her man? If not God, then who? She spoke none of this, although the priest who stood and looked at her dark death mask of a face may have read this blasphemy through the anger flashing in her eyes. He guessed the truth of Walter's suicide, but seeing how the pain had shattered both these women, decided not to add to their distress. In any case, he was too exhausted to argue. "We will bury him this afternoon. Will you come?"

Katherine shook her head. "I will send some money for the burying," she said woodenly.

The priest turned and left, his shoulders bowed and weary from the pain he saw around him – from the grieving, frightened eyes of young parents whose babies he had been burying all week. Katherine wondered, for a moment, if there was anyone to minister to this grieving priest, who needed to be strong for so many others.

The dreadful question "Why?" hung over the priest as it hung over Katherine and Maud, as it hung over the nation when people had the courage to ask it. "God, what have we done that you would treat us so?" Katherine had shouted this question over and over in her mind. Now she screamed it through the mouldy, rain-soaked roof and into the sky. "What have we done? What is our sin that carries such a penalty? Do you want me to follow Walter into the Wensum?"

Maud stood by, hard, angry. Desperation carved its familiar lines across her face. She had lost her grandchildren, the tiny gifts that gave her life and hope. But her mother's need to comfort her suffering daughter was stronger than her own despair. She stood beside Katherine for a while and let her scream her rage against God. Then she put her aching arm around the pain-racked body of the only love she had left. There was a stiffness in their embrace, and Katherine tried slightly to break away. But Maud held her, loving her devastated daughter even through the aching of her own despair.

Sister Joan heard the women screaming anger in their hut. She waited outside until the sobbing stopped. Then she went inside, but said nothing. There was nothing she could think to say. She put some water in a pot and blew on the fire to bring it to flame. When the water boiled, she made them a brew from her favourite herb, Saint John's Wort, and bade them drink it. She returned every few hours, brought them food, and gently touched them on the shoulder or arm. "Here," she whispered. "Drink this. It will help."

It kept on raining, day after day – a low, grey, drizzling rain that only wetted the misery that hung over all of Norwich, as it hung over all of England...a misery they called "the children's pestilence," because it mostly took children born after the first pestilence...small ones, little ones, who had no time to sin, and so must have died for the sins of their elders. But why?

Then finally one morning, sunshine sparkled on the grass. Sister Joan, after she had made her brew, coaxed Maud and Katherine to eat some fresh baked bread and suggested that they walk outside in the garden. Too weak to resist, they went out with her into the sunlit garden. "Sit here on this bench," Sister Joan said quietly, "and let the sunshine heal you. I'll come back to get you soon."

The sunshine did its work. When the nun returned, the women were walking around the garden, talking quietly about the herbs and flowers. Sister Joan smiled and turned to do her weeding.

Healing doesn't happen in a day or week or month. The gaping holes of cold depression that such tragedy cuts into a soul are never healed, but if the tears are not suppressed, if the anger is not buried, each passing day blunts the edge a little more. One day when Sister Joan came into the hut she saw Katherine and Maud looking at the book. Sister Joan had seen it there, and had been curious, but knew she'd need to wait until her questions could be heard above the pain.

"It was given to me by my husband's father on his deathbed," explained Katherine. "I learned to read a few words of Latin from the sisters here at Carrow when I was a girl. But I can make no sense of these words at all."

Sister Joan looked more closely at the book. "It's in the English tongue," she said.

"English!" Katherine and her mother were astounded. "A book in English?" And then they laughed, far more laughter than such discovery would warrant, but laughter from the same place in their souls that made their tears. And then suddenly the laughter turned to tears.

Sister Joan put quiet hands on their shoulders. She knew there was still much weeping to be done, so she said nothing. She didn't urge them to stop. But when their tears began to ebb she asked them, "Will you come with me into the chapel?"

Red-eyed, still sobbing, too weak to protest, they went with Sister Joan. She motioned them to kneel with her at the altar rail. "Look," she said, pointing to the crucifix above the altar. "Look at your Lord. See the blood on his brow and the pain in his face. He was abandoned by his friends, and in the end, he felt abandoned by his God. 'My God, my God! Why have you forsaken me?' That's what he yelled when he was hanging there and hurting, dying. He knows your agony, my sisters. He knows your suffering." Then, silently, Sister Joan rose and left them there.

Katherine held her mother's hand and gazed up at the suffering Jesus. She blinked her eyes to focus through her tears. The two women stayed there kneeling, hardly thinking, hardly praying.

Suddenly, just for a moment, Katherine was sure she saw fresh drops of blood welling from the wooden forehead. Was it a mirage? Was it somehow, beyond knowing, a reality? Katherine remembered wishing, as a girl, to be fully in the presence of the crucified Christ, so that she could enter more fully into his pain and sorrow. She sobbed out loud, "But oh Jesus, not this way – not through the dying of my children and my man."

Still, day-by-day, they healed each other – mother and daughter, with the help of Sister Joan. Tears there were, and bursts of anger. Each day they found themselves back kneeling in the chapel, looking at the bruised and battered face of Jesus. And sometimes, words began to form in Katherine's mind, words that came somehow from the crucifix, but not through sounds. In her heart she heard, "Daughter. As you come to know my pain, so also you shall know my joy."

One day when Sister Joan came to offer her daily ministrations of fresh-brewed Saint John's Wort, aromatic fresh bread, and kindly touch, Katherine asked about the book again.

"You say this is English, Sister? I never knew that words on parchment could be English. I thought books only showed the Latin words of Holy Church, or the French words of the nobles. Can you read this English?"

"Some perhaps," said Sister Joan. "Like you, I've only learned to read some Latin words from the breviary, though I often don't understand their meaning. The priest who comes to say our mass tells us the Latin tongue most truly speaks the mind of God."

"Will you read me some of this one?" Katherine asked.

It was slow going. Sister Joan sounded out each syllable, each word. "The letters of the English make the same sounds as the letters of the Latin," she said. After a long struggle and much laughter, the three women had read one whole sentence. "A mighty fullness of spiritual comfort and joy in God moves into the hearts of those who say or devoutly sing the psalms as an act of praise to Jesus Christ."

"Maybe this is a book about the Psalms," said Joan excitedly as she left to attend to other duties.

Katherine read and reread that sentence, working to fix the shapes of letters in her mind, because she suddenly sensed that reading was the key, the key to – what? To life perhaps?

It took a full week to read the first page, but read it she did. Slowly, one letter, one word at a time.

Katherine and her mother and sometimes Sister Joan puzzled their way through, word by single word, though sometimes there were words they'd never heard before.

The next page came more easily, as did the next, until Katherine found herself reading whole sentences without needing to stop and puzzle the sound and meaning from a word. Her enthusiasm and excitement grew.

Then one day Katherine realized that Sister Joan's first guess was right. "It is!" she squealed to her mother. "This *is* a book about the psalms from the Bible!" In fact, she discovered it was a commentary on the Psalms by an eccentric Yorkshire monk named Richard Rolle. Not only had this brilliant, passionate mystic interpreted the meaning of each psalm, he gave the Latin line, and then its English translation. So Katherine learned a little more Latin as she learned to read her native English, growling when she hit a word she could not understand, or when the same word was spelled in several different ways. "Just to confuse you," Maud laughed.

Sometimes words leapt from the page, words that named the pain and loss that still consumed her through the cold, dark nights that would not set her free. "How long, O Lord? Will you forget me forever? How long will you hide your face from me? How long must I bear pain in my soul?" The words, Katherine knew, were ancient and it gave her comfort to know that she was not the first to feel such agony, such loss. Others had walked her painful path before her. It explained nothing, but it eased the hurt a little.

Late one night Katherine began to wonder if this book, for her, at this time, was chance or destiny. She concluded it had somehow been the work of God that brought her to this book, but then the rage welled up within her as she thought how God had done this. "God, if you wanted me to read this book, did you have to kill my children and my husband to accomplish it?" She slammed the book down on her table and paced in the garden until dark. Still, she was back studying her book the next morning as soon as the first light of day made reading possible.

"I've asked the priest at Saint Julian's to write a letter to your brother," Maud said one day. "We've not seen Thomas since I gave him to the Benedictine brothers at the cathedral priory just after you were married. Perhaps his prior will give him leave to come and see us."

Thomas came to visit two weeks later. He was tall and gangly. Katherine found him almost comical, his youthful hair a ring of tousled straw around his tonsure, his blue eyes dark and tired, his loosely fitting ankle length gown too large for his thin, still childish frame. But Katherine didn't laugh or even smile, so badly did she want to love this brother she had hardly known or seen since her marriage to Walter. Would she have recognized him had she seen him on the street, this thirteen-year-old brother she had been a mother to? She wanted so much to hold him close the way she held him as a child. But Thomas struggled hard to carry the demeanor of a priest in training, so Katherine only shook his hand.

"I can stay one hour," he said, his face flushed with embarrassment. "I can come and visit you one hour each year, if it is convenient to Father Prior." Then there was silence. Neither he nor his mother or his sister knew what to say. It seemed as if a whole lifetime separated them, which indeed it did.

"What is your work in the monastery," Maud asked, trying to get a conversation going.

"Our work is the *opus Dei,* the work of God," he said, trying hard to sound mature and official. "We gather in the choir seven times each day, according to the Rule of Saint Benedict. We rise at midnight to sing the night office, and that is followed by the *lauds* of the dead. We sing *prime* early in the morning. At mid-morning we sing *terce*, *sext* at midday, and *none* in the mid-afternoon. *Vespers* comes at the end of the afternoon and *compline* at dusk. That is our principal work. At other times I am a student, learning to read and write in Latin, and to study the works of the church fathers."

The two women knew all this of course, but they listened respectfully, though Katherine found it hard not to smile a little at his not quite successful attempt at gravity. Again there was silence and again Thomas blushed.

"Can you teach me how to make words on parchment?" Katherine said in a burst of enthusiasm that surprised them all. She was searching for a task to bridge the years that had them standing there like strangers.

Thomas blushed. "I wonder why a woman should want to learn such things." He tried to sound official, but his voice croaked, revealing his thirteen-year-old uncertainty.

"Women have made letters, and they have made books," said Katherine. "Saint Hildegard of Bingen, I have heard, made books. Please teach me, Thomas."

"You mean you would write your own words?"

Katherine hesitated. "No, brother. I have a book here. It was given to me, a legacy from my husband's father. I want to copy it and make another book which I would then give to you." It was an impulsive thought. Katherine wondered why she would even think of such a task.

"Benedictines are not permitted to own anything, though it is true some older monks and priests own things. *I* would never ask for such permission!"

"Then I will make a book for you," said Katherine, her enthusiasm growing. "But I will not give it to you till you are priested and permitted to own it. And anyway, it may take me many years to do such a long work. I am a feeble and unlettered woman. But teach me what you can, brother."

They had no quill or parchment. But Maud brushed aside the rushes that covered the dirt floor of their small hut, and found them a sharp stick. Together, brother and sister knelt on the floor and mother sat and smiled, enjoying her two children together. For the first time since the great pestilence she felt the inner glow of motherhood.

"Notice how the lines curve around each other," Thomas said importantly. "Study the shape of each letter. If you had a quill to write with, you would bear down slightly where the lines are broader, and thus you would have a pleasing shape, not only in the letters, but in the lines that make the letters. The written words must be clear and a joy to read, but they must also be a thing of beauty in themselves."

Thomas clearly enjoyed the role of mentor to his older sister. And Katherine found herself enthused about a new challenge that was shaping in her mind. When her children and her husband died, she had stumbled toward Carrow, not knowing why but only that she had to go there. Two months had come and gone and she had not gone back to the tannery.

Suddenly she stood up tall. "Thomas," she said, her voice breaking with excitement. "On your way back to the priory, go by the house of Uncle Robert. When I was left a widow, he hired men to run our tanning trade. Thank him for his kindness. Then tell him I wish to sell it now. He may buy it if he wishes, or he may sell it for me. Tell him to bring the money to me here at Carrow Abbey."

"What are you thinking, Katherine?" Maud looked worried. "Have you decided to take the veil?"

"No, mother. I don't feel a call to be a nun, at least not yet. I just want to learn." Katherine paced around the hut in her excitement. "Sister Joan says there is a large library of fourteen books here at Carrow. I want to buy a corrody and live here with you. And then I will ask the Mother Abbess for permission to spend my days there, reading books and learning how to copy them." Then she hesitated. "Do you think I'm mad, Mother?"

Thomas interjected. "You are not mad, Katherine. But, well...I think you are not wise." He saw the question on Katherine's face. "Well, ah, women are the weaker vessel, and some priests question whether women have souls," Thomas continued, blushing again. "Women should be wives or nuns. And Saint Paul said women should be silent and leave matters of religion to the men."

Maud sensed an argument developing. "Thomas," she said quickly, "your hour is almost over. Katherine has asked you to stop by Uncle Robert on your way back to the monastery. And when you get back, ask your prior if you might not come more often than once a year to visit. You have given your life to the church, but surely God can spare you more than one hour a year. Ask if you can come more often."

When Thomas was safely out of earshot, Maud spoke. "Katherine, Thomas is right. What you are proposing is most unusual."

"I know it is, Mother. But can there be harm in learning from the words of those church fathers just as Thomas is doing? Can there be harm in learning how to copy those words so that more people may read them?"

"Katherine..."

"I know. I know. I'm a woman. I will have no thoughts of my own, Mother. I simply want to read what the sainted masters have written."

"But you do, Katherine. You *do* have thoughts of your own. You always have had. As a child you had the same fantasies and dreams that other children had, but you built on those dreams and imagined things other children could never understand. Even *I* couldn't understand them."

"Mother, no! I..."

"Listen to me, Katherine! When we sent you here to Carrow for a year of learning how to read the liturgy, you came back full of ideas and dreams. You have a very agile mind, Katherine, and the road you are proposing could be very dangerous to your spiritual health, and perhaps to your very life. You are, after all, a woman, as Thomas says, and not equipped to think such high thoughts."

"I know. You're right, Mother." Katherine stood, her shoulders drooping. Then she straightened. "But I have to do this! I have to!"

Maud and Thomas were simply expressing the common view and there seemed to be no arguments against it. Katherine herself agreed that women were the inferior sex, not suited to lofty thoughts or difficult considerations. But still, for the first time in her life, Katherine felt a sense of call, an urgency – to stay at Carrow, to learn to read and write.

She spoke to Sister Joan, and through her arranged an audience with the Mother Abbess. The abbess, the Reverend Mother Cecily, was not the wizened old matriarch Katherine had imagined. She was older than the other nuns, no doubt, but there was fire in her grey eyes. "What can I do for you, child?"

Katherine bowed politely – nervously. She had her speech well rehearsed.

"I am a widow, Reverend Mother. I lost my two children and my husband short months ago in the return of the pestilence. I came here to grieve with my mother, Maud, a corrodian here. I inherited my husband's tanning trade and my uncle is selling that. There will be enough money to buy for me a corrodian so that I can stay here with my mother. And from that there will be money left so that I may make the abbey a small gift. From my late father-in-law, I inherited a book about the Psalms, which I wish to give to the abbey. I have learned to read that book and it inspires me to read much more. And to learn to copy such books. I therefore beg leave to sit in the library here at Carrow, to learn what I can from the books and to teach myself to copy such books so that others may read also."

"Sit down, child," said the abbess. "Do you wish to take the veil, to become a bride of Christ?"

"No, Reverend Mother. At least not now. I don't have the sense of vocation to become a nun, though that may come with further study of the books here at Carrow."

"You say you have taught yourself to read? Latin?"

"No, Reverend Mother. The book I have is in the English tongue, though strangely different than the English that we speak here in Norfolk. But the book also has Latin in it, and the English words for the Latin, so I have learned a little."

"But you taught yourself? You had no teacher?"

"Sister Joan, yes, at the beginning. She helped me read the first few pages. I came here to Carrow for one year mostly to learn a little

Latin for the mass."

"I doubt you learned much. Or at least, when *I* went to a convent school as a young girl, the sisters seemed to enjoy punishing us. *Vae natibus*, woe to the buttocks."

Katherine smiled. "We must have gone to the same school."

"They're all like that. So, other than the nuns and Sister Joan, has anyone been helping you?"

"My young brother, Thomas, who is at the priory, has helped a little." Katherine hung her head and blushed. "Mostly I have been teaching myself."

The abbess looked at her intently. "Why do you want to read books, child?"

Katherine wished the abbess wouldn't call her "child." "I hope I am not being too brash in saying this, Reverend Mother. But I feel deep inside me that God is leading me toward these books."

"Sister Joan has told me some things about you. She tells me you and your mother still harbour a deep anger against God for taking your loved ones. Is that true?"

"Yes, Reverend Mother." Katherine could manage nothing more than a whisper. "And I have wanted to confess that sin, but I cannot until I am truly repentant. I shall go back to my hut and meditate and pray for grace to ask forgiveness."

"No, no, Katherine. Do you think God is a vain, arrogant despot who doesn't understand the pain and anger that we feel when someone we love has died? You have been reading the Psalms. Have you not read the anger, the rage, that King David in the Psalms flings at God? Even Jesus on the cross threw angry words from the psalms at God. 'My God, my God, why have you forsaken me?' Did you see that in your book, Katherine?"

"I have read that psalm, yes, Reverend Mother."

"If God can bear the anger of a psalmist and of Jesus, God can surely bear the anger you and I can shout." The abbess reached over and took Katherine's hand in hers. "When you are ready, make your peace with God. All your life, Katherine, all your life, you will find pieces of that anger in your soul, but God will give you grace to hold that anger and that pain in your hand and offer it as a prayer for those you loved so well."

Katherine was crying now. "Will the books tell me, Reverend Mother, why God kills our loved ones? What are the sins that demand such terrible justice?"

"No, Katherine. They won't." The abbess scowled. "They offer answers, yes, but their answers won't satisfy you. They haven't satisfied me. I am not convinced that God sent the plague, especially not as punishment, even though we've heard that tortured wisdom spoken from the pulpits." The abbess stood and walked toward the crucifix that hung above her kneeling bench. "Punishment is an answer that comes from the hearts of men who know too much of the ways of war and kings and power, the ways of reward and retribution. My heart tells me God is not a cruel despot, but I have not the skill or intellect to argue otherwise." She turned back to Katherine. "Perhaps you will someday."

Katherine looked up. The abbess was smiling. "Yes, that means you have my blessing. Read all our books and learn to copy them as well. I will arrange a spot for you in the library where you can read and copy books whenever the light is good enough. And I'll arrange for parchment and quills and all that's involved in writing. But I grant this with one condition. You must come and talk to me once each week to tell me what you have been reading, and what you make of it."

Her first impulse was to hug the abbess, which she knew would be quite improper. Smiling through her tears, Katherine took the hand the abbess offered, then turned and ran to find her mother.

Maud complained that Katherine spent almost every daylight hour in the abbey library. "You'll go blind from so much reading." So Katherine tore herself away from her books and came back to her hut each day just before noon to share in the main meal of the day and to walk the gardens with her mother. Or if the weather was bad, to sit inside their little hut and talk.

At first Katherine was deeply discouraged. The books in the Carrow library were all in Latin, and it took her days to read a single word or phrase.

But Katherine worked long and hard to learn the ways of her new vocation. Slowly, painfully, she learned to read the Latin books she found in the abbey. She read each page as often as she needed to, often checking back to Rolle's book to see if the word had been used there in another way.

She had no dictionary to look up meanings. No resources at all, except her visceral determination to find out what the words were saying. And this meant going back again and again over passages, until the context made the meaning clear. Daily she quizzed Joan and any other nun who knew any Latin at all, but they were seldom of much help. Often she waited till her weekly visit with the abbess to ask the meaning of a word. Even then, there were many times when the abbess couldn't help her either.

Fortunately, Thomas managed some visits. Every month or so he'd find a few hours and get permission to come. The two of them would then pore over books together. Thomas had much better facility in Latin than she did and Katherine enjoyed nothing more than to be taught by her younger brother. And at every visit Thomas complained – it was almost a ritual – that "women should not engage themselves in such conceits as reading holy books."

Sometimes, Katherine fairly bubbled with excitement over the ideas, the thoughts, the insights she found in the books. "On the other hand," she told her mother, "I fall asleep at my reading when the fathers just go on and on and use so many words to say such simple things."

One day, Katherine came running out to get her mother. She took her hand and pulled her into the library. There they gasped in awe at the beauty of an illuminated psalter, a book of psalms with the first letter of each poem intricately and colourfully designed. Carefully, they turned the pages, studying and marvelling at the lines, the brilliant colours, the sheer joy expressed by the unnamed artist.

Both women had heard that monks would spend many days working on the design and the colouring of a single letter to open the chapter of a book. But they had never seen such beauty before. Katherine wondered if perhaps they saw this illuminated manuscript more keenly because of the general drabness that characterized the rest of their life. Their clothing tended to be grey or dark brown, houses were small and never painted though the occasional one might be brightened with a lime whitewash. There was little light inside most buildings.

Only in churches was there colour and beauty and a sense of vitality, especially in the cathedral. That is why Maud insisted that Katherine walk with her to Norwich Cathedral from time to time, to wander around on the cool dirt floor where people stood in worship, to gaze at the sun streaming through the stained glass windows, to run their hands along the smooth marble forms of the statues, to have their spirits lifted by the high and graceful vaulted ceiling.

Once when Thomas walked the cathedral with them, he told them of the bosses, the carved figures placed where the ribs of a vaulted roof are joined. "In the cloister where we walk when we go to sing the hours, we pass beneath the images of Christ in his crucifixion, and then we see a most wonderful carving of Christ in judgment, with the old law on one side and the new law on the other."

"Can we go see them?" Katherine asked eagerly.

"No. Only priests and monks and seminarians are allowed in the cloisters." He saw the disappointment in his sister's face. "I have heard Father Prior say that someday such bosses will be carved for the roof of the nave as well."

Katherine and Maud encouraged Thomas to talk about his life in the monastery. "Do you find it hard to wake up in the dark to go to *matins*?" Maud asked.

"Oh, no! It is a joy to wake up and go to worship God." Thomas saw the skeptical look on his sister's face. "Well, sometimes, yes it is hard. Especially in the winter when it is so cold, and we have to stand there in the dark and sing."

"Is there no light at all?"

"Only one candle for the one who is to read. We know everything else from memory."

—

Eventually – though it took several years – Katherine read the books in the Carrow library: Augustine's *The City of God*, writings by John Chrysostom, and Bernard of Clairvaux. She found great delight in the story of Saint Bridget of Sweden. And when she read *The Fire of Love*, by Richard Rolle, it seemed as if she'd encountered an old friend.

There was one book she looked at often. "I don't want to begin reading it until I know my Latin much better," she told Maud. It was the Gospel of Mark. Except for the illuminated Book of Psalms, it was the only portion of the Bible the abbey owned.

—

Maud couldn't seem to hear enough of what Katherine found in her books. Sometimes it seemed to her that Katherine was living a dream she vaguely remembered, because the sparkle in her daughter's eyes brought the old fire back to her eyes too. But never was there an adequate answer for the question that lurked in the dark corners of their lives. "Why? Why does God send or permit such things as the pestilence?"

Maud bought a wax slate for Katherine on which she could practise her letters, rather than waste expensive parchment. And the two of them discussed the shape, the size, the form of every letter. They puzzled over words together. "Why don't you try writing, Mother?" Katherine asked.

Maud was blunt. "I'm an old woman and I have no will to become a scribe to copy the words of dead men."

"But it may be," said Katherine, "that you have words of your own you'd wish to write."

"Foolishness, girl! Sheer folly. I am old and ignorant, and I am a woman. I have no words to write that anyone would want to read. You may have such words to write, though they'll get scant respect because you are a woman. God does not intend women to do such things."

Slowly, Katherine taught herself to write. From large words scratched on the cottage floor, to smaller letters pressed awkwardly into the wax slate, until finally the courage to use expensive parchment. She began to copy, one letter at a time, John Rolle's book of psalms. At first she could only write a word or two before her hand and arm began to ache, but steadily over the months – punctuated by splotches of ink and tears of frustration – she learned the writing of her own English tongue, even when Rolle's Yorkshire dialect baffled her.

—

Katherine's life cycled between joyful discovery – new ideas in the books she read, the illuminated manuscript, the beauty of the cathedral – and deep depression. The melancholia began always in the darkest hours of night, especially when the winter clouds hung low and cold. She would wake and feel the gloom surrounding her, seeping into her belly, refusing to be dispelled, no matter how she concentrated. Drizzling rain, that often continued day after dreary day in the winter, seemed to ache its way into her bones. Then she would simply sit. She ate and drank a little when her mother cajoled her into it. She answered in single words when her mother tried to start a conversation.

Maud brewed the Saint John's Wort as Sister Joan had instructed her and sat beside Katherine until she drank it.

Then, one fall day when Katherine was deep in her depression and neither Maud nor Sister Joan could move her, help came from a most unexpected source – a tall, awkward, muscular teenage girl named Alice.

"Mother Abbess told me to bring her here," Sister Joan said to Maud. "When you paid for your corrody, it included the services of a maid, and all this time there's been none. This girl's name is Alice. She has run away from a most degrading and sinful situation. She needs a place. Mother Abbess says she can be your maid if you agree. Her manners may be rough, but you could teach her better. You may beat her as much as necessary to make her obey."

Maud stammered, hardly knowing what to say. "We don't really need a maid, but if she needs a place, ah..." She looked at Alice, big, bony, muscled, almost crouching like a cornered animal, ready to run or fight. "We won't hurt you, Alice."

"Please, ma'am," Alice spoke in a tiny, fearful voice. "I need a place. Strong as a fartin' ox, I am. I'll work my little arse off for yez."

Sister Joan snorted slightly, put her hand across her face and left. Maud didn't laugh, but her eyes teared up and she couldn't talk for a few moments. Even Katherine turned from her gloomy corner and managed a slight smile.

"Well, Alice, you can stay for a while until we see how we get along. Would you like some of this vile potion that Sister Joan makes us drink? It tastes awful, but it does help one feel better. Here. Come sit down at the table. Are you hungry?" Maud moved a loaf of bread closer to her.

Alice's hands shook as she took the brew – shook from fear, from hunger. She wolfed down the bread as if she hadn't eaten in weeks. Maud sat down with her and told the trembling Alice about herself and Katherine and why they lived at Carrow Abbey. "There isn't a lot of work to do here, Alice. There's the rushes on the floor to be replaced sometimes, and wood to be chopped for the fire. We get our food from the abbey kitchen, so there's no real cooking to do. Clothes need to be washed every month or so. Maybe you could help Sister Joan in her herb garden."

Maud wondered how such a physically strong woman could be so frightened. Several days later, when Alice seemed more at ease, Maud asked for her story. "Who are the enslavers you've run away from?"

"Ma'am." Alice sounded just a little more relaxed. "You would scarcely want to hear my sorry tale."

"We'll need to know it, Alice. Because if you have run away from something, we must know what it is so that we can either protect you from whoever enslaved you, or return you to them."

"Ow! Ma'am! You wouldn't have the heart to return me to them people. Say you wouldn't throw me to them howlin' wolves!" Alice began to weep loudly.

"Alice. Stop that," said Maud firmly. "I won't tolerate that kind of caterwaul unless I know you have something to howl about. Tell me your story."

Alice sniffled loudly, put her thumb up against a nostril, blew, and wiped the mucus on her sleeve. Katherine was sitting upright now and listening, which was a sign that her depression was lifting.

"Well, ma'am. It was that whoreson Hugh who runs the Bishop's brothel up by Poke Thorpe Gate."

It was true, Maud knew. Brothels were often owned by bishops, who considered prostitution a necessary evil – and a convenient way to earn extra funds. Men, they reasoned, needed somewhere to rid themselves of evil sexual urges. A regulated brothel was the answer. But they were regulated only to protect their customers. There was nothing to protect the poor young women who had no other place to go. They were brought in, used until they sagged too much to interest their clients, then discarded and left to die. For homeless peasant girls who had no family, no money, prostitution was the only alternative. Both marriage and the convent usually required a dowry.

"I run from the whorehouse, because the whoremaster told me I was as ugly as a hog's arse. The men folk that come by didn't want me no more, he said, less'n I did other things for 'em." Alice began to cry again. "They wouldn't let me do just normal humpin'. They wanted me to do things even dogs won't do. So I run. And I come here, and the Mother sister said maybe you'd let me be your maid. I can work powerful hard, ma'am! If you send me back to that whoreson Hugh, I'll jump in the Wensum River just like some of the men did after the pestilence."

Katherine snapped to attention. "Tell me about the men who jumped into the river, Alice. Do you know their names? Tell me!"

Alice recoiled in fear and looked to Maud for protection. "Don't be afraid, Alice. Just tell Katherine what you know."

"Well, I don't know their names, ma'am. Not usually. But some there was that made me cry, they was so sad. I never knowed why a man goes to see a whore when he's hurtin', but that's what they do. One man there was, who come to me, but he just set there in the corner, not even takin' his pants down. I'm sitting there naked as a jaybird waitin' for him. I says to him, 'If you come in here for some fun, sailor, let's get at it.' And he just looks at me, and the tears come up in his eyes, and he says, 'I lost my babies. I lost my babies.' And then he runs right out and they say he run and jumps off the Fey bridge into the Wensum. Poor bugger."

"Tell me what he looked like," demanded Katherine.

"Oh, ma'am. I seen so many men, they's pretty much all alike ..."

"Tell me what he looked like!" Katherine barked.

"Well, he was kind of short, and he smelled of a tannery..."

Katherine screamed, then burst into deep, body shuddering sobs.

"I'm sorry, ma'am. I didn't mean nothin.' What did I say?" Alice pleaded.

"You did nothing wrong." Maud put her hand gently on Alice's arm. "You touched an old wound. A very deep wound, and she has to cry it out now. You go out into the garden and help Sister Joan for a while. I'll let you know when Katherine has finished her tears." Maud went to sit beside her daughter, to hold her hand and gently rub her shoulders, as the tears, for now at least, lanced the festering boil of despair.

It was a strange relationship that grew between the three women. Maud, who had become matronly, slightly stout, but quiet and kind. Katherine, a passionate scholar, a bit thin from not eating regularly, who found herself often in conversation with the nuns and especially with the abbess about matters spiritual. The abbess, it seemed, looked forward to their weekly conversations even more than Katherine. "It is too bad you are woman," she said sadly one day. "Because, Katherine, you could be a fine scholar if God had made you a man."

And Alice. Tall. Muscular. Awkward. But now with a small sense of security, a sense of friendship in Katherine and Maud. And friendship, sometimes, even from the nuns who hardly knew what to say to a former prostitute who spoke the language of the street. She began to show a lively personality, a sharp wit. Her language sometimes appalled Katherine and Maud, but more often sent them into paroxysms of laughter.

Which was all the more a miracle, because Alice should have been angry and morose and suicidal, considering the life she'd had. Gradually, as she felt the trust of her new guardians, Alice told her story.

"I was put out when I was a baby, ma'am. That's all I know."

Although she didn't say it, Maud knew that unwanted babies were often abandoned on church steps, or outside the homes of wealthy families. It was not usually spoken of, but neither was it condemned. It was a convenient way to dispose of unwanted children. Most babies born out of wedlock were usually welcomed into the extended family, or valued at least for the work they could do. But there were children born under embarrassing circumstances, such as the children of priests, or sometimes to upper class women who had a reputation to protect or a clandestine affair to hide.

Usually the priest baptized the baby quickly, then took it to a foundling home. If the children taken to such institutions survived to about the age of six, and most did not, they were usually placed – sold might be the better word – to a family that wanted a child for the work it could do.

"All I remember," said Alice, "is the farmer who come and took me from a place where there was lots of children. I don't remember a whole lot. But I remember walkin' beside the cart and the farmer was ridin' in it, and it seemed like such a long way till we come to a barn, and they made me live there. I got to sleep in the straw beside the cows.

"They left me bits of bread and pots of gruel or some other slop. I had to get it all inside me real fast, because them rats would eat it. And I worked near every day, from sunup to sundown – diggin' in the fields, gatherin' nuts and fruit. If I snitched any of that fruit the famer would whop me good with a stick. I was powerful hungry most all the time.

"That farmer and his wife were drunken folk. Most every night, they'd fall into bed pissed as a newt. So that's when I'd sneak into the house and steal some food from the whoresons.

"As soon as I growed a bit after a couple of winters with the farmer, that whoreson started grabbin' me and makin' me lie down in the bush so he could hump me. Every couple a days he'd do it, and sometimes he hurt me real bad."

"Did the farmer's wife know about this?" Maud asked.

"She found out, soon enough, and started callin' me a vixen, a slut, a whore, and told him to take me into town and sell me to the whoremonger."

"I'm sure life in the brothel was even worse for you," Maud said gently.

"Sure. Yeah. The whoremonger made me and the other women drink some green stuff every month if we wasn't bleedin' when we should be. And then I'd bleed so bad I couldn't hardly stand up, and I'd puke like a dog."

"Why does God allow such sin?" Katherine asked the abbess one day. "Poor Alice was thrown to the dogs the day she was born. Her only victory is that she stayed alive. We call what she has done a sin, and yet until she ran away to come to us, she had no choice. She was a slave."

"We are born to sin," sighed Mother Abbess. "You have read Saint Augustine's book, no doubt?" Katherine nodded. She noted that Abbess Cecily spoke more with resignation than conviction. "Augustine explains how it is that the sin of Adam, who gave in to the temptation of Eve, is visited upon us. We are conceived in sin, and, except for the loving mercy of God, we die in sin. Women are the worst afflicted. It is through our bodies that we tempt men to sin. That is why we try, in our monasteries and convents, to purge our sinful bodies, to mortify our flesh, and to pray without ceasing, that we may become more worthy of God's mercy in the life to come."

The abbess paused and sighed. "At least that is what we are taught, although there is a voice deep down inside of me that says it is false."

As she knelt in the chapel that evening, Maud on one side, Alice on the other, Katherine tried to frame a question. Or was it a protest? It seemed stuck inside her, and all she could do was pray: "Lamb of God, have mercy on me, a sinner."

Her unframed question, her unresolved anger, her recurring depression drove Katherine repeatedly to the books she now began to love and cherish, even though they often confused her even more and made her angry.

Three years after she had run to Carrow Abbey, Katherine had enough Latin and enough courage to begin reading the one book she so badly wanted to study. The Bible – the *Vulgate* – the Latin translation people believed had been made by Saint Jerome in the late fourth century. The abbey did not own a whole Bible, just Mark's gospel and the illuminated copy of the Psalms that had so delighted Katherine and Maud. The entire Bible was a collection of many books, and only the wealthiest cathedrals, universities, and abbeys owned a complete set. Katherine wondered why the Bible was not written in her own English, but when she asked the abbess, her response was one of horror. "God's word is written in God's language," said the abbess.

Neither the abbess nor Katherine knew that in Oxford a group of scholars was gathering around a man named John Wycliffe, a controversial cleric who had the protection and support of John of Gaunt, Duke of Lancaster, the son of King Edward III. They had begun work on the first English translation of the Bible.

Eagerly, Katherine began her reading of the Gospel of Mark. "There are four accounts of the life and death and resurrection of our Lord," explained the abbess, "but Carrow has only this one. The monks at the cathedral have all the Bible, but they will not let women read from them."

"Not even a nun?" asked Katherine.

"Especially not a nun," said the abbess. "Though they would never admit it, they fear us greatly. We tempt them and lead them into sinful thoughts, they say, and sometimes sinful acts. I do not know how we do this, but that is what we are taught, and that is what we must believe."

Katherine knew that anything taught by Holy Church could not be challenged, especially not by a young, unlettered laywoman. But she challenged them in her thoughts, and wondered if that was a sin.

Every day she poured over the Gospel of Mark. "Before all things, the Gospel of Jesus Christ," it began. She found herself drawn to the book, to the story of John the Baptizer, the calling of the disciples, the parables, the miracles, and how Jesus took a small child and placed it among the disciples and said, "If you welcome a child in my name, you welcome me." Katherine wept when she read that. She still had tears for her dead children, but now the tears came freely, and when they came they cleansed and liberated.

Katherine found more tears as she read for the first time the story of Jesus' crucifixion. It was a story she had heard told many times and seen dramatized in the mystery plays. But somehow in the reading the story came strangely alive to her. Even though the hour was late and the light was fading, Katherine did not stop until she read the words of the Roman soldier saying, "Certainly, this man was the Son of God." As Katherine walked slowly in the twilight through the abbey grounds toward the hut she shared with Maud and Alice, she remembered the prayer of her childhood, for the sickness unto death and to enter into the pain of the crucifixion. "Why would I have such a prayer?" she whispered into the gathering darkness. "How could I bear such pain if my prayers were answered?"

It took Katherine many days to read the whole gospel. As was the custom of the time, she read out loud. Her Latin improved day by day as she worked, but she could only guess at many pronunciations. It was laborious and slow. When she read the final words, she clapped her hands and laughed, as she read how the risen Christ had spoken to the disciples – how the risen Christ had worked with the disciples and told them to proclaim this wondrous news.

When she had struggled to the end of Mark's gospel, she began again at the beginning. She read it much more easily now. And then a third and forth and fifth time, each time more easily and with deeper understanding.

Then she decided to copy it herself. She was surprised how quickly the skill of copying in Latin came to her. Using the same letters she had mastered writing English when she copied Rolle's book, she soon found herself able to write down whole verses without looking back at the original manuscript. Still, it took her a month to complete the copy, partly because she could only work for an hour or two before her hand began to ache or the light faded.

Mother Abbess didn't altogether approve of this project. She cautioned Katherine. "Copying a book in English is one thing, or even copying one of the books of the church fathers. But copying the Latin text of a gospel may not meet with the approval of the learned fathers at the cathedral priory. I can fend them off as long as we don't speak too much of it. Don't tell anyone, especially not your brother, what you are doing. He might tell his abbott and that could mean trouble. I wouldn't talk about it too much with the nuns here at Carrow either. It is not forbidden for a woman to copy a gospel, but it's not particularly approved of, either."

"Thank you, Reverend Mother."

"It would be best if you did not show this copy of the gospel to anyone. It is, no doubt, full of errors."

Katherine winced. She didn't think so. She had been very careful. She took her copy of the precious gospel to her mother's hut each night, wrapped it in cloth, and placed it out of sight. Long before she finished, she had decided on her next project. The Book of Psalms. She did not aspire to paint the elaborate illuminations of the copy in the abbey library, but she could copy the words. As she relished the thought of this new challenge, Katherine realized that her times of depression – the long, long nights in her prison of despair – were fewer and shorter. "I must remember to thank God for that in my prayers," she whispered to herself.

Katherine wondered how it could be possible that she enjoyed these solitary times so much – how these quiet times alone with her books and her thoughts and her prayers enriched her soul. Her mother worried that Katherine was always in the library or in the chapel, or sitting by herself, absorbed in thought. More and more, as the years followed one upon the other, she found the solitary life to her liking.

Every morning, at least for the main meal of the day, Katherine joined her mother and Alice. "She is the salt of the earth," Katherine said to her mother one day. "Alice could not tell a falsehood even if she wished to do so." Much as the brutality of her life showed on her body and sometimes in her words, there was an innocence about her eyes that Katherine and Maud had grown to love.

"They look like chicken scratchin's," said Alice one day when Katherine showed her some writing. In fact, Katherine wondered if she should teach Alice how to read, but then decided no, because God, too, must love her honesty and innocence, and chuckle sometimes at her earthy speech. All those serious thoughts might spoil her. The thought surprised Katherine. Was it possible that God might chuckle, might laugh at such earthy innocence? Then Katherine remembered the Gospel of Mark, and Jesus' injunction to welcome children in his name. "He surely must have meant such children as our Alice," she thought.

Gradually, Katherine began to draw on the wisdom of this child of sorrow. Their friendship deepened until one day Katherine found the courage to raise again the matter of Walter's visit to Alice.

"Oh sure, I remember him easy," said Alice. "Your man, he come to me hurtin' bad. It was all over him. Most of 'em who come into me was hurtin' or they was drunk. Or both. The drunk ones was mean and dirty. Sometimes they's so drunk they can't get it up, and then they'd slap me around as if'n it was somehow my fault. But the hurtin' ones, what they want is lovin'. They want a mama to hold 'em and rock 'em, and sometimes they let me do that. Sometimes they is so hurtin' or so lonely. Just like your man. He was hurtin' so awful bad, he couldn't hack it no more."

"Our two babies," said Katherine. "He had taken them to the priest to be buried. He loved those children – he loved them so deeply, though he couldn't ever say it. And I think he loved me too, in his own way. We never talked about love much, Alice. I wish we had. Why is that, Alice? Why don't people speak to each other about love?"

"Men got the idea they gotta be tough and strong, and they don't need nobody to hold 'em and love 'em. Half them guys comin' to the whorehouse really was lookin' for someone to hold 'em close. They didn't really want the humpin' but they couldn't think of no other way of gettin' up close to someone."

One day, as Katherine sat in the library thinking deep and terrible thoughts about a God who loved children, yet killed them in a plague, Mother Abbess came to her. She brought a book called *Ancrene Wisse*, the Guide of the Anchorite. "You may find this useful, and if you wish, you may copy it for me."

She offered no reason. No explanation. She handed the book to a surprised Katherine and left. Katherine had heard about the book, but had not seen it in the Carrow Abbey library. She had heard of anchorites, although there were none in Norwich at the time. Immediately, Katherine sat down and opened the book. It was in English. "Thank goodness!" she muttered. Katherine realized how tired she was of reading Latin, which often seemed so cold and detached. English had much more vitality, more verve and passion.

But the *Ancrene Wisse*, she soon discovered, was punctuated by Latin throughout. The writer, not named anywhere in the text, was writing for "my dear sisters," evidently anchorites already. "A book written for women," thought Katherine, finding herself surprised and a little pleased at the idea.

It spoke of two rules. The first is "for the heart and makes it even and smooth without the lumps and pits of a conscience crooked and accusing." The second rule is for the "body and bodily deeds. It teaches everything about how one must conduct oneself on the outside, how to eat, drink, dress, sing, sleep, wake."

"How did you come to have this book?" Katherine asked the abbess during their weekly conversation.

"When I was young, I felt God call me to the life of an anchorite. My father wanted me to marry and had promised me to a man he knew. It would have been a good alliance for him, and would have made our family more powerful and wealthy. Father was furious when I said I had a vocation to become an anchorite. There was much loud argument, lots of shouting, and finally my mother proposed a compromise. Well, it really wasn't a compromise. But it made my father feel he hadn't entirely lost the argument. So I came here to Carrow as a novice. Many years later, after I became abbess and had a bit more freedom to move, I bought this book from the monks across the street from Saint Julian's. I have never read it."

"Why?" Katherine was incredulous.

"I think I was afraid. No, I am. I am still afraid. Sometimes when I rise from my aching knees after singing *lauds* in the darkness, I yearn for the life of solitude, of prayer, of study, of reflection – the life of the soul and the life of the mind. I think it would hurt too much. That book would make me discontent with my life here as abbess."

"Why did you give the book to me? Do you want me to become an anchorite?"

"What *I* want for you doesn't matter a whit. What does God want for you? And an answer to that question will only come to you in prayer." The abbess paused, then reached out and took Katherine's hand. "Are you praying, Katherine? I know prayer was very hard for you and your mother. I don't think God blames you for that."

"Yes, I am. And my mother is too, though she still finds it hard to pray for herself. Time, and prayer, the ministrations of Sister Joan, and God's grace have done their work. We are healed as much as such pain can ever be healed."

"When you've finished reading the *Ancrene Wisse*, Katherine, come and talk to me about it."

Reading this book was slow work. Katherine had eventually found some level of comfort with Richard Rolle's Yorkshire English. But this *Guide for Anchorites* had been written more than a hundred years before her time, by a monk probably from the Herefordshire or southern Shropshire region. His language was substantially different from the Norfolk English that Katherine spoke. And so she struggled with many words, reading out loud. Nor did she find the book always agreeable. She argued with the pious monk, thinking his demands for such extreme piety and self-denial were unnecessary and sometimes silly. "God created me and my body," she found herself thinking one day. "God took on our human body in the person of Jesus. Why then do we need to punish these bodies so?"

But these were private thoughts. It was accepted wisdom that the way to salvation was through the subjugation of the body, literally beating it into submission. Only by humiliating the flesh could the human spirit come into the presence of God.

Katherine read the book eagerly, sometimes finding gems of wisdom that she would read over and over. "Sometimes Our Lord plays with us like a mother with her little darling – runs away and hides, and lets him stay on his own and look anxiously about, and call 'Mummy, Mummy.' Then, with arms spread, leaps out laughing. She cuddles and kisses him and wipes his eyes. So it is that sometimes when God seems absent, we are not loved any less."

An anchorite, said the unknown author, is like Mary, in the Mary and Martha story told in the Bible. When Jesus came to visit them, Martha bustled about preparing a meal while Mary sat at Jesus' feet and listened to him. Martha complained to Jesus that Mary was making her do all the work, but Jesus said, "Martha, Martha! Mary has chosen the better part."

"To be a housewife is Martha's part," said the *Ancrene Wisse*. "Mary's part is quietness and peace from all the world's noise, so that nothing may hinder her from hearing the voice of God. Martha's work is to tend to the needs of the household, and that is also worthy work. Let her be. Mary should not be at all concerned with such things."

But an anchorite, Katherine discovered, does not spend her whole life in prayer and contemplation. She is to observe the daily cycle of seven times of prayer, as they do in the monasteries and convents, but she is also to be a guide and counsellor for those who come by the window of her cell. She is to hear of their pain and offer them her wisdom and her prayers. An anchorite is to do some useful work with her hands – embroidering vestments for the clergy, or if she can read and write, copying books.

It was not an unusual occupation, and it was highly regarded. Most towns of reasonable size had an anchorite. Katherine wondered why there was none in Norwich. More women than men became anchorites, and the majority were laypeople, not nuns or monks or priests. They were a public necessity. The rationale was simple. If God hears our prayers and responds to them, then it is necessary to have people specifically designated to pray. People need to be able to bring their problems to someone who is fully in touch with God. They need more than a priest who hears confession and prescribes a penance. What's more, people also need someone to hear their heartache and offer them guidance.

Katherine tried to imagine herself as an anchorite. The quietness. The time for prayer. Would there be books to read? She enjoyed copying books. She set the idea aside, convinced she had neither the discipline nor the call to such a vocation. But she was surprised how often the conversation turned to anchorites whenever she talked with Maud or the abbess.

And Sister Joan would give her such penetrating looks whenever the subject came up.

1373

God showed me a little thing,
the size of a hazelnut
in the palm of my hand,
and it was as round as a ball.
I looked on it and wondered,
"What may this be?"
And this is the answer that was given to me.
"It is all that is made! It is the whole of creation!"
I was amazed that such a thing could last –
why it did not crumble into nothing.
"It lasts and ever shall,
because God loves it.
And so all things
have their being in the love of God."

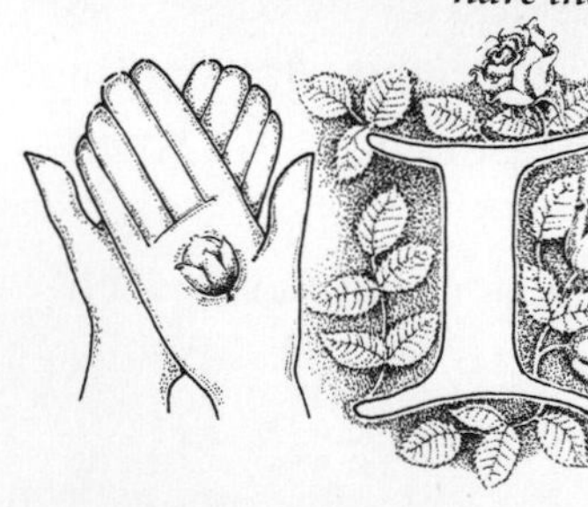

It was nothing to worry about. Sometimes the stronger herbs in Sister Joan's garden gave her the sniffles. She may have had a slight chill.

But toward evening, Katherine's whole body began to ache. Her mother gave her worried looks and insisted that she lie down with a cool, wet cloth on her forehead. She fell asleep quickly. But it was not a restful sleep.

Mixed-up memories of childhood troubled her dreams – of kneeling by the altar of the church, looking up at the image of a crucified and bleeding Jesus. Within her dream she prayed, prayed that she might stand with Mary Magdalene and others at the foot of the cross, feeling in herself the shuddering pains that racked the crucified Christ. "Jesus!" she heard her childhood self cry, "If what I want is what you want, then please let my prayer be answered. But if not, then don't be angry. Don't be angry! Don't be angry. Please!" Katherine saw her childhood self folded in fetal agony at the foot of the cross, and mourned for the child that never had a childhood.

Katherine slept fitfully through the night, and woke in the cold, damp morning to see her worried mother at her side holding her hand. "You were dreaming," Maud said. "How do you feel?"

"May I have something to drink?" Katherine's voice was thin and shaky. Her hands trembled as she drank the diluted ale, then immediately heaved it all into a pot her mother had thoughtfully placed nearby. Maud gently wiped her daughter's face and forehead.

"Mother? Do you remember how Joan and I used to go to church together when we were small? Do you know what we were praying for?"

Maud shook her head.

"You were so angry at God then, Mother. And I was afraid God would kill you because you refused to pray." Katherine tried to raise her head, but then fell back weakly on to her pillow.

Maud gently wiped her daughter's fevered forehead, before she answered. "The priest said God sent the plague to kill your father and your brother and sister – that God killed all the people in the wars and in the plague because we had sinned. I couldn't imagine any sin that deserved such punishment. I still can't. I still don't understand why." She dipped the cloth in the water and gave it an angry squeeze. "But I have forgiven God and I believe God has forgiven me."

"I thought you would go to hell, Mother, unless I did something that would please God so much that you could be forgiven. Joan and I would pray in the church" – Katherine stopped to gasp for breath – "after all the people had gone. I asked God to help me find out what it really felt like, what it must have been like for you to suffer so. I thought maybe if I could know how you were suffering, then I could pray your prayers for you."

Katherine closed her eyes and Maud wondered if she had drifted off to sleep. "But then, Mother, I began to wonder what it must have been like for those who stood by the cross when they killed Jesus. I asked God if I could stand beside Mary Magdalene and Jesus' mother. I thought if I could feel what they felt, then somehow Jesus would listen to my prayers."

Katherine saw the tears in her mother's eyes. Maud had no words, but she held her daughter's hand up to her cheek. Katherine's voice was weak with fever, as she stumbled on through her confession.

"I asked for more than that. I asked that I would get so sick that you and everyone would think I was dying. I wanted to be so sick that you would call the priest and ask him to give me the last rites of the church. When I told Annora about that, she asked God for such an illness too, but I don't think she really wanted it. I really wanted it, Mother. It made sense to me then. I think…it's so long ago, I'm not really sure anymore…but I think I wanted to practise dying, so that when my time came to really die, I could do it in a way that would bring me closer to Jesus."

"Enough for now," said Maud. "Rest for a while."

"No there's more, Mother. I have to tell you this."

"Later, dear. When you feel stronger."

"Mama, no! Please! I have to tell you this now. I don't know why, but I have to. Maybe because, if I die…" Katherine paused to regain her strength. "There's another thing I asked God for, when I was praying there with Annora – with Sister Joan – but I didn't tell her about this one. I asked for wounds, Mother. I wanted to hurt enough so that I could really understand. So I asked for a wound that would help me really be sorry for the wrong things I had done. And I wanted a wound that would help me experience the kind of suffering that Christ suffered. And I wanted a third wound, a wound that would help me really look for God, to really want God with all my heart."

Katherine fell silent.

Maud was crying softly. "You've been carrying the burden of my anger around with you all these years, haven't you? I'm so sorry, Katherine."

"No, Mama. I haven't. I forgot about my first two requests. I didn't really think about them until last night, in my dream. But I've had the last request, for the three wounds, on my mind ever since I first prayed for them. Especially since Walter and the two children died. For a while I thought their dying was the three wounds. Sometimes I was so angry at God, and other times I wanted so badly to be close to God. It doesn't make sense."

"No," said Maud, her voice croaking. "None of it makes much sense."

There was silence between the two women and Katherine drifted off into an uneasy sleep. Her fever rose and Maud bathed her daughter's forehead almost continually. Sometimes Katherine would call out in her sleep, but Maud could make out none of the words.

Sister Joan came round as she often did and shook her head in worry as she saw Katherine's uneasy sleep. She left immediately and came back an hour later with two poultices in her hand. "Put these under her arms," she instructed Maud. "They will draw off some of the harmful humours in her body."

Maud could not say they made a difference. Katherine's fever raged and Sister Joan tried other poultices, with other herbs. She tried to get Katherine to drink some of her warm herbal brew, but Katherine could swallow nothing.

The fever burned for three days and nights. Then Katherine's eyes suddenly flew open. She stared wildly, regaining consciousness just enough to say, "I'm dying, Mother." When Sister Joan came back, Maud met her at the door. "Send for the priest. Quickly!"

As Maud returned to the bedside, Katherine's eyes were beginning to focus. "Help me sit up," she croaked. "I need to sit." Maud frowned, but slid her arm beneath the feverish body of her child, then moved some folded blankets underneath and let her down again. Katherine remained conscious, but she was clearly not better. Her eyes seemed fixed and unblinking. She didn't speak.

The priest arrived. "Daughter," he said holding a crucifix in front of her face. "I have brought you the image of your maker and saviour. Keep your eyes fixed on it. Remember who died for you and for me. This will be a comfort to you as you die." Then the priest quietly intoned a Latin prayer, made the sign of the cross on her forehead with oil, and left.

Maud and Sister Joan settled in for the death watch. They exchanged concerned glances as Katherine's breathing became short and evidently painful. Her head rolled from side to side. But then it seemed there was a calmness on her face. Her breathing became deeper and almost normal. Her face showed varying expressions from pain and horror to profound joy.

Was it hours or minutes they sat with her? Gradually, Katherine's face became more settled. It seemed she was sleeping, almost normally. And then she woke. Sister Joan and Maud spoke to her, but she didn't seem to hear them. She seemed to be thinking of something too deep, too profound for words, and yet several times she tried to speak.

By the time the priest arrived, her eyes were more focused and she was breathing more normally. "You're alive!" he said in astonishment. Then moving very close to her, "How are you feeling, daughter?"

"I've been raving, Father," said Katherine. "I've been raving mad all day."

"Don't let it worry you." The priest laughed heartily. "The devil torments our minds when we are sick, but you have lived. You will be well again soon."

"The strangest thing was that the crucifix you put at the end of the bed – it was bleeding. Enough to soak my bed!"

The priest's expression sobered instantly. Katherine saw it and her lower lip began to quiver. "I think maybe I'm being stupid. I think I've just been really stupid."

"Would you like me to hear your confession now?" the priest asked.

Katherine took a deep breath, thought for a moment, then sadly shook her head. "Later."

Sister Joan came to Katherine's side as the priest went out the door. "You should have said your confession, Katherine. It is always good to cleanse your soul, especially at a time like this."

"Why would a priest believe me, Sister? Even *I* didn't believe what was shown to me by God." Katherine's eyes filled with tears. "Just leave me to be quiet for a while. I have much to think about."

Through the evening she lay there, her eyes constantly watching the flickering flame of the single candle that lit the room, until around midnight she fell back into a troubled sleep. Her mother and Sister Joan slept on mats nearby, exhausted from their long vigil.

"Benedicite Dominus!" Katherine sat bolt upright. "Is everything here on fire?"

The two women rushed to her side, glancing around them to see if there was a fire. "No! No! Katherine, there is no fire," said Maud. "Nothing is on fire, Katherine. It's all right. Just go back to sleep."

"Thank God," said Katherine, falling back down on her pillow. "I thought the devil was trying to choke me and I could smell the stink of sulphur burning. It...Mother, it...smelled like the tannery."

"Nothing is burning," said Maud. "Everything is just fine, and you are going to be just fine. Now try to go back to sleep. You need all the rest you can get."

Katherine closed her eyes, but she didn't go back to sleep. She soon heard the regular breathing of her mother and Sister Joan. The candle guttered and went out. All was darkness in the room, but there was a brightness, a warmth in Katherine's soul. What was this she was feeling, experiencing? What was the meaning of the vivid dreams, or visions, or hallucinations or whatever they were that happened when she was deliriously ill?

In the purple darkness, Katherine could see a city, or so it seemed. And the city was her soul; it was part of her being. And in the middle of the city she saw Christ, beautifully robed, sitting in splendour, and she knew as profoundly as it is possible to know anything, that Christ had made his home inside her and that he found her soul a most pleasing and comfortable home. At that moment, she knew that all the visions she had experienced during her illness were given her by God and that they were a gift – a gift to be treasured. And Christ was saying words to her, words she couldn't hear, but the message was clear. "Katherine. What you experienced today was real. Accept that. Hold on to it. Believe it. You will not be overcome. You shall not be overcome."

Katherine whispered the words into the darkness. "You shall not be overcome."

And then she slept.

Again the dream came. The devil was back, and with a stench so disgusting, so vile, like the fermenting vats in the tannery, like the stink of hell in the mystery plays. She could feel the heat of this devil's body. She heard a kind of chattering – a kind of talking – as if two people were muttering to each other, but she couldn't understand a word of it. The stench and the chattering went on all night long, and then suddenly, as the first light of dawn began to filter through the window, they were gone.

Katherine sat up in her bed and brushed the hair from her face. "I shall not be overcome," she whispered. She sat there and watched the bright rays of sunlight filter through the oiled linen window into her room. She crossed herself, took a long slow drink of diluted ale from the cup she found beside her bed, pulled on some clothes, and walked silently into the morning.

The dew sparkled on the garden as Katherine made her way unsteadily down the path. A jewelled cobweb joining branches of a hazelnut tree showed tiny rainbows in each droplet – reminding Katherine of the Noah story and the rainbow promise made by God into the generations. Blood-red roses entwined through the hedgerow, their petals and thorns shining in the holy stillness of the spring morning. And in her heart, the fire of faith burned bright and warm.

From the ground below the tree, Katherine picked up a hazelnut, mouldy and bruised after a winter on the ground. She held it in her hand, and flooding back into her mind came a memory of the vision she had seen in the depth of her illness. Katherine rolled the nut in the palm of her hand, remembering that dream.

She heard the soft sound of steps behind her. Maud was walking down the garden path, a shawl in her hand, which she gently laid on Katherine's shivering shoulders. She looked down at the hazelnut in Katherine's hand, then to her face.

"Mother," said Katherine in a voice hardly above a whisper, "God showed me something small, round and frail, like this hazelnut. And I wondered why I was seeing this. Then an answer came. There weren't words, but I understood why I was looking at such a tiny thing. It is all that is made, Mother. Everything is there in this tiny creation that could crumble into nothing so easily. But I knew it would last, because God loves it. It has its life, its being through the love of God. God made it. God loves it. And God keeps it."

Maud took her daughter's arm and walked her slowly toward a small bench near the roses. "Creation is such a small thing," Katherine said. Then the two women sat in silence together while the first soft breeze of the morning brushed the dew from the roses beside them.

"You and I are part of that creation, Mother. Just like this hazelnut, God is our maker, our lover, our keeper. But we can never really know what that means until we are united with God the way this hazelnut is part of God." She fingered the nut gently. "That is why we are created, Mother. To be one with God."

Off in the distance, a lark began its morning song. Carefully, Katherine put the hazelnut back onto the ground. "Help me walk back to our house. I need to sleep some more. I'm very tired."

In the days that followed, Katherine slept and ate and talked about her dream, and slept and ate and talked some more. She had to say it all, to speak the words, to fix them in her memory or she would lose the gift, the dream, the vision that seemed to vibrate through her very being. Maud and Sister Joan sat in awe, in fear sometimes, as the stories of the visions came tumbling out. There seemed no end to them.

And then when she had told them all, sometimes several times, she fell silent. Sister Joan and Maud began to exchange concerned looks and urged her to eat, to drink the brew that Sister Joan concocted. Katherine walked around the house and garden, speaking just a single word here and there, her face alternating between joy and a kind of blankness.

"Mother Cecily would like to see you," said Sister Joan "She is waiting for you."

"Why?" asked Katherine woodenly.

"She didn't say. Come. I'll take you to her."

"Sit, my dear," the abbess said. "You are feeling better after your illness, I trust?"

"Yes."

The abbess reached into the pocket of her habit and put a hazelnut in Katherine's hand. "Tell me about the hazelnut."

Katherine stared at the nut.

"Katherine," said the abbess sternly. "I want you to tell me about the hazelnut."

"It's just a nut."

"It is not. God spoke to you about something small as a hazelnut, Katherine. Now tell me what God taught you. Tell me!"

Startled, Katherine began slowly, reaching for words at first, but gathering momentum and passion, until it all came tumbling out, the meaning of the hazelnut, visions of the suffering Christ, the pain, the horror, the glory, the passion, the gift. For hours she talked while the abbess smiled sometimes, nodded, sat up in surprise, creased her forehead in concern.

When Katherine finally stopped, the abbess looked at her in wonder. "Oh, Katherine!" was all she could say.

"I don't know what to do now."

"What do you mean?"

Tears formed in Katherine's eyes. "I was so excited, so elated about the visions and all that God seemed to be saying to me, but now I don't know what to do with it all. I have all this in my head, in my heart. After I told my mother about the vision of something small as a hazelnut – and it was so beautiful and so tender and joyful there in the garden – I thought my life was fulfilled. I lay down to sleep and I was sure I would die then because my life was complete and I would become one with God. But I didn't die. So why – what does God want me to do?"

"Have you prayed for an answer?"

"Yes. Many times."

"No answer?"

Katherine shook her head. "I don't want to go to my Uncle Robert and ask him to find me another husband. My heart is still with Walter and my children. I can't go back to the tanning trade – that's been sold and I don't have the heart for it in any case. Mother Abbess – should I become a nun?"

"No!" the abbess shot back quickly. Too quickly. She reconsidered her reaction. "Dear Katherine, I shouldn't have spoken so impulsively. I wasn't thinking." She closed her eyes as if looking for some inner wisdom. Or perhaps a memory.

"I've never told this to anyone, Katherine. When I was much younger – much younger than you are even, perhaps fifteen winters – I too had a gift such as yours. Not through illness, but on my knees in prayer. The visions were sharp and clear, and I was certain God had spoken to me, directly. That's when I felt called to be an anchorite.

"My father was furious when I told him of my vision. 'Hallucinations,' he called them. 'Ravings.' They had marriage plans for me. But I was strong; I was adamant; I would not give in; and eventually, as I think I told you, we reached a stalemate. My mother suggested a 'compromise,' and so they brought me here to Carrow Abbey. I have been here ever since."

The abbess rose from her chair and paced around the room. "And Katherine, the vision faded. When I became a novice, and then a nun, I found myself in an endless round of work, study, cooking, cleaning, gardening – work and prayer. Long hours of prayer every day and in the night, long hours of work and study, and then exhausted sleep. The way to holiness for a nun is to silence all the noise, all the passion that churns around in our mind – to silence it with prayer and work. Tame the lust of the body and the passion of the soul. And so my vision died. I can scarce remember now what it was that God revealed to that young girl on her knees in church. But as you talked, I found some long-hidden memories. And some anger, yes. Anger that my holy dream has faded into scraps of memory."

The abbess was standing by the one window of her cell, looking out toward the garden. She seemed suddenly much smaller, frail, and bent over with a widow's hump. "I was called to the cell of an anchorite. Instead, I found myself imprisoned by this convent." She turned and walked toward Katherine. Placing both hands on the younger woman's shoulders, she managed a broken whisper. "God has given you a pearl of great price, Katherine. You mustn't lose it."

"I know, Mother Abbess. But I don't know how to hold on to it."

"You must write it down!"

Confusion swirled through Katherine's mind. "I am a woman, Mother Abbess. My brother, Thomas, keeps reminding me of that. Women do not waste parchment with their midnight ravings. Women get married and bear children, or they become nuns or whores. . ."

"Katherine! You would not be the first woman to write her vision. There have been others. Have you heard of Mechtild of Magdeburg? Hildegard of Bingen? They even say that many years ago there was a woman, Joan was her name, who became a pope for a few years until they found her out and killed her."

Mother Cecily's voice gathered anger as she spoke. "It is men, bishops, clerics, schoolmen – men, not God – who have ordained that women must be wife or nun or whore. Some women – your mother for instance – have learned a craft and worked it. Some women have become anchorites."

A heavy silence hung around them as the abbess paced around the room struggling with her emotions while she gathered her thoughts. "I think now I know why I gave you the *Ancrene Wisse* to read. And that thought comes as a surprise to me. And no doubt to you, Katherine."

"No, the thought is not a surprise." Katherine's voice was just above a whisper. "I thought about myself as an anchorite, but I dismissed it because I am much too weak – too indecisive for such a hard vocation."

"Of course you are! But so is everyone else. I was too weak and frail to become a nun. If we rely on our own strength, then failure and disillusionment are guaranteed. But God offers us strength for the journey we are called to undertake. It may be that God will offer you the freedom of an anchorite's cell!"

The old abbess looked at Katherine, who suddenly looked so very young and frail, even though she was by now a woman of thirty. "It is a thought that needs prayer and some time." Mother Cecily walked to the crucifix on the wall above her kneeler. For minutes she stood there with her hands clasped and tears streaking down her cheeks.

Finally, she turned back to Katherine. "Let's do this. You and I will pray about this each day, by ourselves, and then I will meet you in the chapel each day and we will pray side by side. We'll not talk about this again until we have prayed this way for a fortnight. Then we'll meet again and see if God has given us direction."

The abbess held Katherine's hand in hers. Then she kissed her gently on the cheek, turned and stood once more before the open window.

Katherine walked into the strong light of a springtime sun, trying hard not to think – trying hard to wait for God.

1374

God forbid
that you should say or think I am a teacher.
That is not my intention,
nor has it ever been.
I am, after all, a woman.
I am ignorant, weak, and frail.
Even so, I know what I am saying.
It was given to me by
the sovereign teacher.

Katherine had never seen a bishop up close before. She had imagined a man who was old and kind and fatherly and frail. This man came striding to the church of Saint Julian's following a group of beautifully gowned acolytes, one of them carrying a large golden cross encrusted with precious stones. There was incense and singing. The bishop was dressed in his sumptuous robes, and on his head, the resplendent mitre. He was a physically strong man – his neck short and muscular, his eyes cold and dispassionate. The pulsing muscle in his jaw gave the only clue to the bishop's inner tensions. Katherine found herself in fear of this man.

Alice, who was standing well off to the side, had a different reaction. More disdain than fear. She'd never seen a bishop up close either, and didn't really know what she expected. But she didn't like this man very much. "You watch this whoreson," she said to Katherine many days later, "I don't like him a bit. He's pinched like a bull's arse in fly season."

This man was Bishop Henry Despenser, of a powerful family, well connected to the king's household. He'd not earned his bishop's mitre through piety, prayer, and good works. He had not even been a priest or monk before he became bishop. When all the high-blown rhetoric was done, Henry Despenser became a bishop because of family connections, family wealth, and because he had fought on behalf of Pope Urban in Rome. And because his brother was a scandalous favourite of Pope Gregory.

Henry was never pious. But he was popular. He'd captured the imagination of those who mattered – the nobility of Norwich and the wealthy members of the mercantile class. He could ride and he could fight, and he became known as *episcopus martius*, "the fighting bishop." Despenser liked that label. "The church is far too soft," he was fond of saying. "We need more men of iron, strong men with good round knackers. Even though they be priests or monks, they should still be men. Real men, who speak softly, but can wield a club or sword as needed." Despenser, of course, never used a sword. "Thou shalt not smite with the edge of the sword," the Bible says. So Despenser bashed heads with a mace.

The Norfolk gentry liked that. An anxious class they were, feeling threatened by the rising power of the people at the very bottom of the social ladder, the villeins. Ever since the pestilence, the gentry found they had to bargain with these serfs, who demanded better wages and conditions. And it was beneath the dignity of gentry to be bargaining with such human trash. So it was good to have a bishop with some spunk, someone defending the order God ordained for humankind – villeins who worked, priests who prayed, and gentry who fought in wars. A bishop who could fight clearly understood both the priestly class and the nobility, and would protect them from the audacity of these miserable serfs.

None of that mattered just now, of course. The bishop, several priests, and Mother Abbess had gathered for the ceremony. Maud was there. Katherine was surprised and delighted to see her brother Thomas standing off to one side in his still-too-large black robe. His yellow hair was well combed around a neatly shaved tonsure.

Katherine was about to be interred into the anchorhold. The abbess had it built for her on the south side of Saint Julian's Church. She had arranged it all, somewhat over the objection of Bishop Henry. But she had power and Henry knew it.

Henry liked the idea of reestablishing the vocation of anchorite in Norwich. There had been no anchorites since 1313, though they were common in other parts of England. But he would have preferred a male anchorite. A man could much more easily rekindle the tradition – a man who understood the order of things. But Henry chose his battles carefully and this was not one he was prepared to fight with Mother Abbess. So the thing would be done, as quickly and efficiently as possible.

"Is this the woman to be buried in this anchorhold?" he demanded of the abbess.

"Yes, my Lord Bishop. Her name is Katherine."

"It matters not what her name is. She will be known by the name of the church where she is buried. Stand forward, woman."

Katherine stepped forward – trembling before this man's barked commands – her hands tight around the crucifix the abbess had given her. This was the moment, the moment she had both dreaded and welcomed. From this moment there was no more return than there was return from the grave, and indeed the ceremony the bishop was about to intone was that of burial. "If this had been a man," the bishop thought to himself, "it would have been worthwhile to stage a proper High Requiem Mass."

Fear shook Katherine's body as she realized the import of this time. No more walks in the garden with Alice and Maud. No more possibility of marriage and of children. No more tears and laughter with her brother as they watched the annual mystery plays, which told the story of God's work in this world. Once she entered that anchorhold, she could go nowhere else, for any reason. Ever. Not until she was dead.

"It is your vocation to spend your life here in prayer," the bishop intoned. "You will pray especially for those who come to your cell for counsel. Remember that you are dead to the world. Think often of death. Speak often of death to those who come to receive your counsel that they may prepare themselves for God's judgment."

Katherine tried hard to focus on why she had agreed to this – why she had chosen this most difficult vocation. She had seen death face to face in her illness, and in so doing, found a new way of understanding life. She had seen the whole world, all of creation in something as small as a tiny hazelnut. She had known herself to be a loved and valued part of that creation. She could have become a nun, or remarried, or perhaps even earned a living through a trade. She could have let her vision fade into mere fragments of memory, but that would have been to destroy the treasure she had been given. And Mother Abbess had counselled; "You have a gift to share. You can share it best if you become an anchorite where you will have time to write your vision, write it down, and think and pray about it, and share your vision with the troubled souls who come to you for counsel."

In the end, it all came down to this. Katherine had not chosen this vocation. It had chosen her. At the end of all her prayers, at the end of all her long and rambling conversations with Mother Cecily, at the end of all the agony of decision, she had no choice.

This was her new vocation. And it was good.

Katherine would be dead. She had already received the last rites of the church, and now needed only to be buried.

Julian would live!

But was she strong enough? Did she really have the faith she had professed to Mother Abbess – faith to give her life to prayer and solitude, and to the counsel of those who came seeking it? Could she give up everything in order to have...everything? How could it be that she felt both joy and fear?

There was no turning back. The service had begun – the service for the burial of the dead.

"'I am the resurrection and the life,' saith the Lord. 'He that believeth in me, yea though he were dead, yet shall he live. And whosoever liveth and believeth in me shall not die for ever.'" This was all in Latin, intoned by the bishop, who seemed slightly bored by the whole process.

The bishop sprinkled a handful of dust on Katherine's head as she knelt before him. The abbess draped a plain grey cloak around her shoulders and kissed her gently. Then the abbess led her to the doorway of the anchorhold. "I cannot go inside with you, my child. But God will go with you. God *will* go with you."

Katherine was left outside.

Katherine was dead.

Julian stepped into the anchorhold.

The bishop closed the door with a heavy slam. Julian heard the metal screech as he shot the bolt to lock it on the outside. It was done. "I commend thy soul to God the Father Almighty, and thy body to the ground. Earth to earth, ashes to ashes, dust to dust, in sure and certain hope of resurrection to eternal life, through our Lord Jesus Christ, who shall change our vile body, that it may be like to his glorious body, according to the mighty working whereby he is able to subdue all things to himself. In the name of the Father, the Son, and the Holy Ghost. Amen."

Silence. Then, through the heavy oak door, Julian heard the mumble of conversation as the bishop and his party walked back to his palace.

She was alone now. Utterly alone. Was God really here with her, or had God gone with the bishop to his palace?

Julian sank to her knees, the crucifix still tight in her shaking hands, and trembled a prayer too deep for words. She stayed that way through the rest of the morning, through the afternoon, and into the night. Her knees screamed in pain and she longed for sleep – to rest – for she was deeply, utterly weary. But Julian stayed on her knees till she fell asleep in the middle of a prayer and woke up hours later lying on the floor. She crawled painfully to her sleeping mat, where she slept until late the next morning, and was awakened by a gentle, persistent knock at the window to the adjoining room.

It was Alice. They reached out to each other through the window and wept for joy, for sorrow, for old times, for whatever it is that makes sisters out of friends. "Mother Abbess sent me here," Alice sniffled back her tears. "I'm gonna be your maid."

"Alice, that's wonderful! The abbess said she'd send a maid to cook and care for me, but I never for a moment dreamed it could be you." Then her face fell. "But what about my mother."

"No need to worry!" Julian noticed that Alice was red-eyed, and much too cheerful. "It's a short trot from here to the abbey. I'll sleep in this here little room, but I'll wiggle my backside over there each day to make sure Maud has the grub and sticks for the fire and medicines and whatever she needs. And Sister Joan will look in on her too. Don't get your neck in a knot, Katherine, your mama will be fine."

Suddenly Julian was sober. "Alice. Katherine has died. I am Julian, the anchorite. I don't know all that it means yet, but something very deep has changed."

Alice's eyes filled with tears. "I know I'm as dumb as a day-old duck about all this. I just don't figure it. I don't know why you want to be holed up here like a mad hermit. I thought I had it figured, but now that you're here, I just don't get it. You let that bull-necked bishop bury you here like a living corpse, but you're alive Kate, or Katherine, or Julian, or whatever the blazes your name is. Get somebody else to cook your swill and empty your thunder bucket. Get somebody who can figure all this religion stuff. I told your ma and I told Sister Joan I didn't know how to take care of no anchorite. I was right." Her voice rose to a shout. "So send me back to the whorehouse, Katherine. There I can do something I understand!"

Julian reached through the window and held both Alice's hands in hers, while Alice sobbed her frustration. "Alice. Even *I* hardly understand why I am here. I only know that this is where I belong, though I really don't know why. We don't have to understand everything, Alice. The only thing I understand is that God is a loving God."

"God doesn't love the likes of me!"

"God loves you, Alice, and God loves me."

"You! Not me!"

"God loves every creature in this world, Alice. I don't know how I know it, but I know that's what God was telling me in all those visions I had when I was so ill. God has called me here, and God has just as certainly called you here, Alice."

Alice sniffled loudly and wiped her nose on her sleeve. Julian smiled at her. "Someday we may understand, but then again, we may never understand. It doesn't matter. We know that we belong here. God wants us here, Alice. Both of us, because I can't do it without you. I didn't know that until just now, but it's true. So we will stay here and try to listen in our prayers to whatever God will call us to."

Alice had stopped sobbing and the makings of a smile crept across her face. Julian reached through the window and took her hand. "I know something else, Alice. I am famished. I could eat a half-cooked rat."

Alice broke into a teary grin. "Don't start talkin' like me, Katherine – I mean Julian. I'm the one that's got to learn to talk right and proper if I'm going to be maid to a flippin' saint."

"Alice, please. Never. Never stop being yourself. I love you just the way you are, with your honest, earthy tongue; a tongue that is wiser than you know. And I never was a saint, I am not now a saint, and I never will be. So get that silliness out of your head. Now, for goodness sake, why are we standing here. Did you bring anything to eat?"

Alice grinned and opened up a small pack. "Mother Abbess sent us fresh bread and cheese. And a bottle of wine. She said the wine was for me, because anchorites ain't supposed to drink nothin' stronger'n ale. But she said I could give you just enough to wet your whistle."

"Wouldn't do for a 'flippin' saint' to get tipsy, now would it," Julian grinned.

"You'll be stuck with watery ale most of the time, Julian. You have to really try hard to get tipsy on that stuff. Oh, and the abbess sent these too. A handful of hazelnuts. She didn't say why."

Julian held the small nuts in her hand and fingered them gently, savouring the memory. "After we've eaten, Alice, I want you to take half of the hazelnuts out into the garden and plant them. See if one of them grows into a tree. I'll keep the rest in my cell here to remind me of God. Now stop talking. Let's eat!"

"In the name of the Father and of the Son and of the Holy Spirit. Amen." The two women spoke the words and crossed themselves automatically, and without further conversation dined as regally and as well as any royalty could wish, passing food and drink back and forth through the window. "Well," said Julian, wiping the last crumb of bread from her face. "We have a lot to talk about, Alice. You and I have to decide how we can live together in this place."

And an interesting place it was. Julian had never visited an anchorite so had not seen an anchorhold. "Some anchorholds are built like a prison," the abbess had once said, "and some are downright luxurious. I know of one anchorhold where there's even a garden for the anchorite to take the air." Julian could tell by the tone of the abbess' voice that such a garden would be unlikely in the accommodation being built for her.

Julian looked around her new home. She smelled the close, damp odour of new mortar. She ran her hand along the flint stone walls, just like the walls of St. Julian's Church to which it was attached. Her room was just large enough to hold a narrow frame with a straw mattress. There was a stool, a writing desk, and a kneeler that stood against the east wall where she hung the crucifix the abbess had given her. There was no decoration of any sort. The dirt floor was covered with rushes, and in the centre was a small pit where, on the coldest days, a small fire could warm her cell, with the smoke rising through a hole in the thatched roof.

There was one door, the big oak door the bishop had slammed to shut her in. Julian had vowed that she would never cross that threshold again. It was a vow she was to keep – or almost keep.

The abbess told Julian she'd had some heated discussions about that. "A priest in the bishop's palace says the door needs to be sealed. But there are many anchorholds where the maid comes into the anchorite's room to tend to her needs. Besides, what virtue is it if you remain in your anchorhold because you are locked in?"

The door led into the room where Alice lived and slept and prepared their food. And from that room a door into a small garden and a path that led to the street, which ran to the south of Saint Julian's Church.

There were three small openings out of Julian's room, each with a curtain that could be drawn across it. One, called a "squint" because it was cone-shaped, narrowed down to a small opening into Saint Julian's Church. Through it she could hear the daily mass, receive the Eucharist fifteen times a year as prescribed by the *Ancrene Wisse*, and say her confession to the priest.

No doubt, that squint was the most important opening, for through it she would receive the spiritual food that would sustain her through the long years in the anchorhold. And each morning she would hear the mass said by the priest at Saint Julian's and meditate on the body and blood of Christ present in the elements of the Eucharist.

But the second window was, it seemed to Julian, also important. A double black curtain was pulled across this window. Between the two sheets of black was a white curtain, and a cross was cut out of the black to reveal the white behind it. It opened into a small anteroom, which had a door on to the street. Those who came to the cell to seek Julian's counsel could come out of the rain and sit on a small stool while they talked.

Julian wasn't sure about the curtain. Some said she should never, under any circumstances, open it. The *Ancrene Wisse* said it could only be pulled back under very special circumstances, and never for a man. The abbess sniffed at this legalism. "Open the curtain when you need to, Katherine," she had counselled. "Until you gain confidence in your vocation, open it seldom if at all. But you will soon see that words tell you only a little of what is in a person's soul. You must see the face. You will soon learn when to open your curtain and when to keep it closed."

The third window opened to the room where Alice lived. Through it Julian received her food and whatever else she needed. And high up on the southern wall, there were two windows covered by oiled linen through which the sunlight could enter the cell. The man sent to oversee the building of the anchorhold had complained to the abbess; "Why would the anchorite need two windows, if she will spend her life in prayer?" In the years to come, Julian was often grateful to the abbess for her foresight.

Julian was delighted to have Alice as a maid, but Alice had very few of the housekeeping skills needed for her new work. She had learned many things since running to Carrow Abbey. She had come to the convent knowing nothing except backbreaking farm work and prostitution. But even at Carrow, her duties as a maid were limited. She cleaned the small hut she occupied with Katherine and her mother and she did their laundry. She went to the nun's refectory each day to collect their daily allotment of food and ale. And she helped Sister Joan tend the herb garden.

But Alice had never cooked anything, never been to the market, much less made a purchase. Even in the brothel, she was given her allotment of bread and ale, and the occasional bit of fish or vegetable. Only on one or two occasions had she actually seen money. "I felt like a priest in a whorehouse," she said when she returned trembling from her first venture to the market.

"Go to Carrow and talk to my mother," Julian suggested. "Maybe she can take you to the market and show you how to do things."

The Norwich market was a fifteen-minute walk from Saint Julian's Church. Maud herself had only been to the market twice before, because for most of her life she'd had a maid to do the shopping and food preparation. The first day out, the older woman and the strong younger one wandered aimlessly, not quite knowing what to do.

It was the noise that met them first. Conversations, arguments, loud haggling over prices, and occasionally in the distance the sound of a tin whistle played by a blind beggar. But the tune was mostly drowned out by the hawkers selling their wares.

"Genuine relics newly brought by pilgrims from Jerusalem! Holy medals blessed by the Holy Father! A vial of the Virgin's milk that will bring you cure from all ill and speed you safely through purgatory into heaven!"

Maud tried to make her way past the hawker of relics, but he blocked her path. "Madam, madam, please consider." The hawker displayed his gap-toothed grin. "I can see by the quiet beauty of your eyes that you are a holy woman."

"I have no interest in your bogus relics." Maud was angry. She tried to push the hawker aside.

"Madam," the hawker oiled his way closer till Maud could smell the garlic on his breath. "I can see you are of noble birth and therefore discerning in such matters. Consider. Here I offer you, for just a few pennies, a piece of the holy cross on which our Saviour died. Think what this could mean for the safety and welfare of your soul."

"There are enough pieces of the cross being peddled about the country to build the king's navy and enough of Mary's milk to float it. Now stand aside!" The hawker grumbled, shrugged, and moved on to seek some less discerning victim.

Then the smells. Rotting meat. Urine. But through the stench, the occasional sweet smell of new baked bread or roasted pork.

The acrid stink of chickens, thin, wet and miserable, lying on the ground, their legs lashed together, while a wizened old man yelled, "Chickens! Fat, juicy chickens!"

"How much?" demanded Maud.

"How much do you think?" the man challenged.

"You tell me how much you want, first."

"A penny a piece," he shot back. A group of women squatting nearby, each of them with their own clutch of ragged grey chickens, cackled with laughter. Maud knew the price must be exorbitant. "Ah!" she said, and walked on.

There were clutches of men and women selling vegetables and

fruits – potatoes, small brown apples, cabbage, turnips, carrots. Further on were the sellers of pungent herbs and medicines, others selling bundles of firewood. Most of the sellers squatted on the ground, their wares in a small circle around them. Some of the wealthier sellers had small booths with a tattered canopy above them. Flies swarmed everywhere, especially around the meat stands. The smell of blood, soaked into the soil and rotting, the stink of rats skittering in the shadows, did nothing to quell the sense of ugliness that seemed to overpower Maud.

"So what did that beast die of," Maud demanded.

"Freshly killed this morning," said the hawker. "A fat, young calf it was too." Again Maud noted the suppressed laughter of the nearby meat-sellers. She turned on her heel and walked off. Alice, who was simply trying to look inconspicuous, followed quickly behind her. The two women walked back to Saint Julian's.

"We're going to have to do this several more times before we discover how to buy things without getting cheated."

"I seen some of them guys before," Alice blurted.

"You mean you know them?"

"I don't know them. I seen some of them before at the whoremongers."

"Did they recognize you?"

"Nah! They didn't notice me then. All they seen was a hooker." Her voice quavered a little.

"It must have been awful for you," Maud said gently.

Alice was suddenly solemn. "I just wanted someone to notice me a little. I know I'm just a foundling. I'm a kid nobody wants. But then when I tried to say something, like a little bit of talkin', they'd just say, 'Shut up, slut. Lie down and open your legs.' I know it's what I have comin' to me for bein' a whore, but jeez, I didn't want to be no whore. An' if that whoremonger finds me, he'll make me go back, cause I guess he owns me. Do I have to go back to the market, ma'am? He goes there lookin' for customers. An' if he sees me..."

The two women walked in silence – Alice still quietly crying, Maud wondering how she could be protected. She acknowledged the class difference between them. Alice was a foundling and a prostitute, although a reluctant one. She may have been born of middle or upper class parents, but she was a villein until proven otherwise, and she quite clearly belonged to the whoremonger who had paid for her. That's the way things were. That's the system God had ordained. Even though she thought of Alice with affection, even with her rough backstreet language, there wasn't much she could do about it. And Norwich was not so big a place, especially since the plagues. Sooner or later the pimp would find Alice. That was inevitable.

"We have to keep going back to the market, Alice," she said finally. "Your duty is to take care of Julian in her cell. And that means you've got to go out and buy your food, or both of you will starve. When we encounter the whoremonger, we'll see if we can work something out. Maybe we can buy your freedom."

They went back the next day, the two women. And the next. And for three days after that, before they made their first purchase. They had some idea of prices now, having overheard more experienced buyers haggle. Alice was too timid, but as the day wore on, she grew more confident. She even gained a grudging compliment from a fishmonger who angrily dropped the fish, for which she had haggled for fifteen minutes, into her basket.

Then she heard the voice. It was a thin, whining kind of voice and she knew it instantly. She wheeled around and faced the whoremonger. His face went red with anger. "You! Slut! You are mine! I paid for you!"

Whack! Without thinking, Alice swung her fist in a furious haymaker, and sent the man sprawling onto the lap of a very large woman selling cod just behind him. The woman swore at the whoremonger and slapped his face with a fish. The marketplace roared with laughter. Alice stomped off in the other direction with Maud scurrying after.

Julian laughed till her eyes watered when they told her about it. "You have come of age, Alice," she grinned. "You are now a woman! That dirty man doesn't own you anymore and I'm sure he knows it."

"When I saw him, somethin' just snapped. I was so surprised, I didn't know whether to shit or go blind. So I whacked him, real good. I rang his bell, for sure. Maybe I shouldn'a hit him so hard."

"Of course you should," laughed Julian. "And if you see him again, just tell him you're going to whack him twice as hard."

Things were very different for Alice at the market after that. She had gained an instant reputation, and everywhere the market regulars greeted her by name and treated her with deference and respect as she haggled with them over prices. And the word was around that Alice was maid to the anchorite at Saint Julian's. "Musta been some kinda miracle, turnin' a dirty slut into a flippin' saint." Alice chose to ignore such comments.

The brothel master was still around, and occasionally repeated his demands that she return to him, but always from a discreet distance. And sometimes Alice retorted with insults to his masculinity. Julian frowned when Alice told her what she had said. "You've knocked him down, Alice. You don't need to stomp on him."

"That lowdown son of a sea cook. I'd knock him down again if I had the chance."

"Alice," said Julian. "Who made you?"

"I don't know, ma'am," Alice said solemnly, feeling that suddenly the conversation had become very serious. "I don't even know who my parents were. The farmer said I was somebody's bastard."

"Alice. God made you. Do you understand that?"

"No, ma'am."

"Alice, you and I have become very good friends in the months since you ran from the whoremonger. I think of you as a sister."

"Oh no, ma'am. I'm a foundling. I'm a bastard. I'm a slut. You're just pissin' into the wind."

"Alice!" Julian was angry now. "Don't you ever talk about yourself like that again!"

"But, ma'am!" Alice was crying. "That's what I am!"

"You are a child of God, Alice! Let me tell you the story of how God made the world. Do you know the song, *Adam Lay A'Bounden*?"

"Yeah," she said tentatively. "One of the women at the whoremongers used to sing it, I think."

"Well, sing it with me."

Adam lay in bondage,
Bound up by a law,
Four thousand winters long,
He never thought at all.

Alice wiped her nose on her sleeve, then joined in on the second verse.

And that was for an apple,
An apple that he took.
That is what the priests
Find written in their book.

Had he not snitched the apple,
Had the apple not been t'ken,
Then never would Our Lady
Have been the Heavenly Queen.

Blessed is the time
That apple taken was.
And that is why we sing
"Deo Gracias!"

"You know, you have a nice voice, Alice. You should sing more."

Alice blushed. "What does *'Deo Gracias'* mean?"

"It's Latin. It means, 'thanks be to God.' Do you know what the song is trying to say?"

Alice shook her head. She could feel a lecture coming and wasn't sure she would like it.

"Alice, in the beginning, before there was anything, God created the world. And God made the oceans and the sky and the moon and the stars, and God made all the animals. And God said, 'That is good.' And then God said, 'Let us make humans in our own image.' So that's what God did. God made human beings, a man and a woman. We are made by God, Alice. We are made in God's image, which means we're like God in some way. And God loves us."

"Is that a true story, ma'am?"

"It is a true story, Alice. A very true story. But there's more. The first man that God made was named Adam, and the first woman that God made was named Eve. And they did a terrible, terrible thing. They disobeyed God, who had put them in a beautiful garden where they would never have to work and never have to know any pain or anger. God told them not to eat the fruit of one tree. They could eat everything else, but not that one tree. But they did anyway. It was the most awful thing they could do. These two humans, made to be like God, were given everything they could want or need. But they disobeyed. And so they had to leave the beautiful garden. That was the beginning of all our woe."

"I don't know about all that stuff, ma'am. Until I got to the abbey, I never went to no church or nothin'."

"Let me finish the story, Alice. When Adam and Eve disobeyed God, all kinds of terrible things happened. And then, finally, God decided to do something really wonderful. Jesus was born, God's son! Jesus was God's own son, Alice. That's in the song. If Adam hadn't snitched the apple, there would have been no Mother Mary, and no Jesus. But it all happened, and Jesus came, and he taught us many wonderful things. He was God's son, and he said, 'Love your enemies. Do good to those who hate you.'"

"Does that mean I have to love the whoremonger?"

Julian decided to ignore the question for the moment. "Jesus was God's son. And he was so good and so holy, the people of his time couldn't stand it. So they killed him. They made him die the most horrible, painful death you can imagine."

"If that was a long time ago, how do you know about it?"

"Holy Church teaches us about it. And I saw the story in the mystery plays every Corpus Christi day. Some of it I read in a book called the Bible. But most of all, when I was terribly, terribly sick – you remember that, Alice? – God sent me a vision of Jesus dying. It was a most wonderful gift, a most beautiful vision of God dying for love of us. I saw the red blood trickle down under the crown of thorns, and I was overwhelmed with wonder that Jesus, so holy and awesome, should care about a person like me."

"You wanted to watch some guy dying?"

"Not 'some guy,' Alice. Jesus. God's son. Years ago, when I was a child, I asked God to send me such a vision. Then I forgot all about it until God answered my prayer. And in my vision I saw him dying. I saw the drops of blood oozing from his head, like drops of rain running off the roof. I saw the pain in his face. I even felt the cold wind that dried out his body. It was terrible and it was glorious. I could almost feel his pain, which is what I wanted."

"Why?" Alice was incredulous.

"Because if I could feel Jesus' pain when he died, I would know how much he loved us. He died that way because he loved us, and I thought that if I could see his dying, if I could feel his pain, I might be able to feel the pain of all the people he died for. People like you. People like that whoremonger."

"He died for the whoremonger?"

"Yes, and for you too, Alice. And when I watched Jesus dying, in my vision, suddenly his face changed and I could see the most beautiful joy. And he said to me, 'If I could do any more for you, to show you how much and how deeply I love you, I'd be glad to do it. I'd die many times for you'."

"Maybe he'd die for *you*, Katherine. But not for the likes of me."

"My name is Julian," she smiled. "And yes, he died for me, but also for you and the whoremonger, and the nuns at Carrow Abbey and all the people in the market."

"Ma'am!" Alice was shaking her head and crying. "Ma'am. I been screwed by every sweating bastard in Norwich. There's no God, no Jesus what loves the likes of me. I know you are a kind and beautiful lady, and I'll turn myself upside down and inside out for you, ma'am. But there ain't no God what cares a pig's turd about me!"

"We'll talk more about this, Alice," said Julian patting her arm. "But for now, do you believe that I love you?"

"I believe you are a wonderful and kind lady, and I don't know why you are being kind to me, but as long as you are, I'll bust my backside for you."

"Well," said Julian, "just try not to be too hard on the whoremonger, Alice. He's just like the rest of us, trying to live in a world that seems terrifying and painful."

Alice sniffed. "I won't hit him no more. But I ain't going to be friends with him neither." She busied herself preparing the food for the late morning dinner. Julian prepared herself for *terce*, the prayers she said and the psalms she chanted each day at mid-morning.

"Kind and most merciful Father; We have erred, and strayed from thy ways like lost sheep. We have left undone those things which we ought to have done; And we have done those things which we ought not to have done; And there is no health in us. But thou, O Lord, have mercy upon us, miserable offenders. Spare thou them, O God, who confess their faults."

Julian's prayer time, as she followed the cycle of seven times of prayer each day, consisted of the Psalms, most of which she now knew by heart in English as well as in Latin. The abbess had given her a Latin breviary, which she kept on her kneeler. Julian spoke the prayers and readings assigned to each of the canonical hours.

The cycle of prayers was a useful discipline, Julian thought. But she needed more. So Julian took time each morning, before the world began to move around outside her cell, to sit or kneel in silence, gently setting aside any thoughts that came along, waiting for the Holy Spirit. She often found this time of inner silence more invigorating than the formal prayers. It was not that words came into her head during these times of meditation, but her mind seemed more clear, more rested, and more able to think creatively after the meditation. In these times of meditation, she was able to lay aside problems she couldn't solve, her concerns about Alice or concerns about others, and sometimes herself, that she could do nothing about.

When Julian rose from her knees, Alice brought a small loaf of coarse bread to the window, along with a few cooked parsnips and a piece of dried codfish she had soaked and pounded for an hour to make edible. All of it washed down with a pint of watered ale. "In the name of the Father and of the Son and of the Holy Spirit," both women intoned. They ate in silence, on opposite sides of the wall, Julian wondering if Alice had any idea at all what was meant by those words – words they repeated so automatically before each meal. "The child knows nothing at all, nothing, about her religion," thought Julian. Then a second thought occurred to her. "Alice is not a child. She is a woman, just as I am. And while she is strong and can knock men down in the market, she is so frail and so simple and so vulnerable."

Julian kept Alice in her prayers all through the day. But there seemed no response – no sense that God had heard. Then, when she rose from her meditation the next morning, it occurred to Julian that God doesn't respond to specific instances. God tells us about love and faith, and leaves us to work it out in our lives. God loves us, as a parent loves a child, but God doesn't treat us like children. We're given all we need to work things out in our own lives, knowing that if we fail, God forgives us even before we ask forgiveness.

Alice's Room Julian's Anchorhold Anteroom

1375

I saw in my vision
that God is everything.
But sin – I did not see you.
When I saw that God had created everything,
I did not see you.
When I saw that God
does everything that is done,
I did not see you.
And when I saw the Lord Jesus in my soul,
I did not see you.
And so, sin, you do not exist.
And I am sure that the people who enjoy sin
will find themselves with nothing in their hands
when they are done.

Two months after she entered the anchorhold the depression crashed in around Julian again. She woke in the middle of the night feeling as if her body had turned to stone. She felt stiff, and angry, and sore. The blackness of the night around her was nothing to the darkness of her soul. Her melancholia, which she thought she'd left behind, had come into the cell with her.

Julian was still lying on her bed, staring at the roof, when Alice opened the curtain. "Ma'am?"

No response.

"Ma'am. What's wrong? Alice opened the door into Julian's room. She knelt beside the bed. "You've got the bleedin' darkness back in your heart, haven't you, ma'am?"

Julian nodded.

Alice got up, blew on the fire in her room, and before long the kettle was steaming. She made Julian a cup of Sister Joan's brew. "Here, ma'am. Drink this. It will help you feel better."

Julian pushed the cup away and stared at the roof.

"Drink this! Right now!"

Startled by the command, Julian took the cup and managed a few sips.

"More!" demanded Alice. "Now!"

Trembling, almost frightened, Julian drank the rest of the dark brown liquid.

"Ma'am," said Alice. "I'm sorry for barkin' at you. But you got the darkness inside you now, and it's not lettin' you be who you really are. Maybe it's an evil spirit or somethin'. Anyhow, until you get rid of whatever it is that's got your tail in a knot, you're goin' to do what I tell you. I don't know who you are right now, but you ain't Julian. So until Julian comes back, I'm in charge."

Julian stared at Alice. Her face hung limp – expressionless.

"All right now. Get off that bed and say your prayers," Alice ordered. Julian didn't move. "Now!"

Slowly, Julian forced herself to her kneeler, and almost inaudibly began repeating the prayers she knew by heart. Alice closed the door but kept on listening through the window. Whenever Julian's voice stopped, Alice shouted, "Keep prayin'."

When the prayers were said, Alice forced another cup of Saint John's Wort brew into Julian, then made her sit and listen to all the latest gossip from the market. Another cup of Saint John's Wort, and then Alice commanded a nap.

For three days, Alice walked Julian through the rhythm of the day, forcing her to say her prayers, making her drink the brew, regaling her with marketplace trivia. She tried, without success, to get Julian to eat something. On the fourth morning, Julian called through the window. "Alice, I'm starved. What have you got to eat?"

Alice squealed her delight. "I've got a king's banquet for you, ma'am. It may look like a hunk of dark bread and a cuppa thin ale, but it's really roast venison and fine French wine!"

"Thank you, Alice," said Julian with tears in her eyes. "I wouldn't have made it through the darkness without you. If it ever comes back again, do exactly what you did this time." Julian managed a chuckle and reached through the window to take Alice's hand. "But get some new stories from the market, Alice. You were starting to repeat yourself."

It was a full month before the first visitor came to Julian's window. Not that she'd been totally alone all that time. Maud and Mother Abbess came almost daily for the first while, sitting in the small anteroom that had been built around the window onto the street, helping to ease Julian into the strange new life she had undertaken.

Julian's first visitor was a tiny, frail old woman, who simply wanted someone to talk to. She spent an hour talking through the closed curtain, telling Julian about her children, a bad lot it seemed, about her neighbours, an even worse lot, and about the two husbands she had outlived. They were the worst of all and had squandered all the money she brought into the marriage. Julian asked the odd question, but mostly she listened. When the woman finally stood to leave, she asked for Julian's prayers.

"And you shall have them, Mother," said Julian. "But you must pray for me as well."

"Me? Pray for you? Sister, I am a widow. I've been ten times pregnant, though only five babies lived. God hears the prayers of virgins, not of tired old hags."

"I am not a virgin and you are not an old hag."

"If you're not a virgin, how come you're masquerading as an anchorite!" The woman huffed and walked out into the early fall rain.

The abbess had advised Julian, when she entered the anchorhold: "When people bring their cares and fears to you, hold them in your heart only briefly. Pray for them with all sincerity, then give them over to God's care. For you cannot hold in your heart all the pain that will come to your window."

And so Julian prayed for the widow – prayed hard, and ended her prayer, "And so I leave her, most merciful God, in your tender care."

But she didn't. Julian worried and wondered all night long, waking from her sleep, praying for the woman again at *lauds*. Somehow Julian felt she had failed the woman, had not shown her the love of Christ, had not said the words that would have sent her away in peace. Even her time of meditation didn't help her give the woman over to God's care. "The first person to come to my window, and I failed her" – she heard the accusing voice in her own head over and over. And so Julian prayed for herself, prayed for the grace to forgive herself and to ask God's forgiveness. Finally, days later, meditating again in the evening, she sensed a load lifted from her shoulders and she fell asleep quickly.

When she woke up to the daylight, she felt a pang of guilt. She had slept right through *lauds*. But then she smiled. Perhaps God had sent her that full night of sleep to ease her soul. Instead of asking forgiveness, Julian breathed a prayer of thanks.

"Besides," she said out loud to herself, "I've got work to do."

Alice poked her head inside the window. "Were you callin' me, ma'am?"

"No, Alice. I was talking to myself. It's so quiet in here, I guess I just needed to hear a voice, even if it was my own. But while you're here – please walk to the abbey and take a message to the abbess. Tell her that Julian is ready to write. Then wait for a reply, because I think she'll send some things with you."

An hour later, Alice was back with a large bundle. "The abbess musta been expectin' this. She had this all packed up and waitin'." Eagerly, Alice opened the bundle and handed the contents through the window to Julian. There was parchment. Far more parchment than was needed, Julian thought. "I don't have that much to say!" As she picked up the bundle of parchment and opened the cords that tied it, a wave of bittersweet memory brought a lump to her throat and tears to her eyes. The sheep hides still carried the faint odour of the tannery.

Carefully, Julian looked at the implements of her new vocation. A lead stylus and a ruler with which to impress lines on the parchment, several goose quill pens, a penknife to sharpen the quills and scrape out the inner fuzz, and an inkhorn, full of deep, black gall-iron ink. There was a scraper for erasing errors, pumice to clean the sheets, and a goat's tooth to polish the parchment.

Mother Abbess had looked forward to this when she arranged for the anchorhold to be built on the south side, the sunny side of Saint Julian's church. In addition to the normal furniture of an anchorhold, she included a good-sized sloped writing desk. And the two oiled linen windows above her desk provided the light she needed. "You have received the gift of visions from God," said the abbess. "You need time and a place to write those down before you forget them. God has chosen you for this gift, Katherine."

Julian pressed lines into the first sheet of parchment, then picked up the pen. She realized she had never written words of her own before. She dipped the pen into the little tub of ink, and held it there, not knowing how to start or what to say.

Alice was watching at the window. "So what are you waiting for? Write some words. I want to see what they look like."

"Parchment is very expensive, Alice. It takes almost a whole flock of sheep to make enough parchment for one book. I have to be very sure to get the right words in my head before I write them on the parchment."

"You could say the words to me and then if you think they make sense, you could write them down."

"All right. How's this? 'I asked God for three gifts.'" Slowly, she wrote down those six words.

"Sure takes a whole lot longer to make the words on the parchment than to say 'em," observed Alice.

Julian spoke the next sentence, even though Alice had left the window. "I wanted to experience Christ's passion on the cross. And I wanted to have a sickness in my body. And thirdly, I wanted to receive as a gift from God, three wounds."

Julian sat for a moment and looked at those words. "I wonder if those who may read this will think I've taken leave of my senses?" She picked up the quill, but laid it down again to still the shaking of her hand. These were her own words. *Her words!* Not words copied from another manuscript, but her own words. What authority did she, a mere woman, have to do this? She forced herself to keep writing.

"I had learned many things about Christ's suffering on the cross, but I wanted more. I wanted the actual experience – the way Mary Magdalene and the others who loved Christ were able to be there with him. I wanted to suffer with him, as did those women who stood at the cross when he died."

Julian was not unusual in asking for this. It was a common prayer. Many were convinced that if they suffered in the way Christ suffered, they would earn merit that would speed them out of purgatory and into heaven. But Julian believed that if she could more fully understand the way Christ suffered and died in his love for humanity, she might also be able to understand his great love and what that could mean.

Julian picked up the quill again. "About the second wish – it occurred to me just once. I wanted this sickness to be almost fatal. I wanted it to be so bad that I would believe I was dying and those around me would believe it too. I did not want to actually die, but to experience enough of it so that I would be ready to die when my time came. And I hoped that would be soon. I wanted that sickness to happen when I was thirty years old.

"I thought of the third wish after someone in church told me the story of Saint Cecilia," Julian wrote. Saint Cecilia, according to the legend, had converted many heathens, so the Romans tried to suffocate her in a bath. When that didn't work, they tried to chop off her head. After three strokes, her head was not severed and she lived for three days after that.

"I was so moved by this story that I asked God for three wounds in my lifetime – the wound of contrition, the wound of compassion, and the wound of earnest longing for God." Suddenly Julian realized that was exactly how it had happened; God had sent her that sickness when she was thirty and a half years old.

Julian stopped from time to time to remember the visions, to remember the dreams, to recall exactly what had happened. And then she wrote until her hand ached and the gathering darkness forced her to stop.

Fear and uncertainty gripped her again. Was she really called to do this? Was this really God's will? Surely she had wanted these visions so much that she had concocted them in her own head. She was right when she told the priest she had been raving. This writing was foolishness! In the morning she would send everything back to the abbess and tell her she couldn't write her visions. It was all childish imagination. Nothing more!

Her night was long and restless. After *lauds* in the middle of the night she stayed on her knees for an hour praying out her confusion. She awoke in the morning from a light sleep still convinced she should send the parchment back to the abbess. But almost against her own conscious will, she found herself at the desk again. "Please, for God's sake and for your own good, disregard the wretched worm, the sinful creature to whom it was shown. Instead, strongly, wisely, lovingly, and meekly think about God, who out of courteous love and endless goodness was willing to give me this vision, which I hope will comfort all of us."

That was all Julian could write that day.

There was only one visitor to her window, a very pregnant young woman who asked Julian to pray that her baby would be a boy, because her husband would beat her if it was another girl. Julian prayed that the woman's husband would not beat her.

The rest of the day was spent in prayer, and simply sitting and thinking, finding she actually enjoyed the nourishing solitude. Then Julian did what those confined to cells had always done. She walked in small circles, around and around.

But the next day, right after prayers, she was at her writing desk again, though the question still bounced around in her mind. By what right, by what authority, do I write these words? Though the question remained unanswered, Julian began to record her experience with more confidence. "I saw the face of the crucifix that the priest held before my eyes, and I saw the scorn Jesus received, the spitting, beating, bruising of his beautiful face. There was more grief and pain than I would ever be able to tell you about.

"Then I saw his body bleeding – hot fresh blood. I saw so much blood flowing from him, that if it had been real blood, it would have soaked my bed. And then, though he did not move his lips, I heard the words, 'This is how evil is overcome.' When I saw how evil was overcome, I laughed, and so did those who were with me around my bed. But I didn't see Christ laugh.

"And then I heard Our Lord say to me, 'Thank you for the way you served me when you were young.'" Julian knew, though she wouldn't write it down, that Christ was talking about the way she had cared for her brother and her mother.

The big question, "Is this from God, or are these my own ravings?" was never fully resolved in her mind, but each day it faded further back into her consciousness, and each day she wrote with more confidence. "After those visions of the cross, the fiend came and tried to take away my visions of the suffering Christ. I was desperately frightened again. The heat and the stench were overpowering. And I could hear a kind of chattering, like a couple of crazy people both talking at the same time. So I fixed my eyes on the cross, and I recited all the prayers and psalms I knew, some of them many times, thinking that if I could fasten myself to Christ, I'd be safe. The voices were there all night long, but suddenly, in the morning, they were gone. Nothing except the stink was left. The fiend had tried to lure me into sin, but had failed.

"Sin! What are you? You are nothing." Julian found herself chuckling as she wrote this. "I saw in my vision that God is everything. But sin – I did not see you. When I saw that God had created everything, I did not see you. When I saw that God does everything that is done, I did not see you. And when I saw the Lord Jesus in my soul, I did not see you. And so, sin, you do not exist. And I am sure that the people who enjoy sin will find themselves with nothing in their hands when they are done."

Julian stopped to think. Does that mean that people do not sin? Of course they do. "As long as we love sin, we are in a kind of pain that is greater than any other pain," she wrote. "But when we love God, then all is well. Even though we may sin sometimes, we are not lost. God has created all of us for love. And when we move away from sin and respond to the love of God, then all is well. God wants us to feel the greatest confidence and pleasure in love. Amen."

Gradually, Julian's life developed a comfortable rhythm. She observed the cycle of daily prayers prescribed for monks and nuns by Saint Benedict, which meant four hours of her day on her knees. At first light each day, she said *prime*. Then she heard mass each morning through the squint into St. Julian's.

For several hours each morning, sitting on her stool or walking around her cell, she prayed and meditated for specific people who had touched her life. Then, following the short office of *terce*, Julian gave herself an extra period of silence. Meditation, perhaps. Trying not to think. Waiting. Simply waiting on God.

She needed this time to clear her thoughts for the next hour at her writing desk – her solitude, and her counselling feeding her reflection on the visions she had those few life-changing days at Carrow. Her writing time was often an hour of struggle, looking for the right word, the most understandable phrase, the best way to help ordinary people encounter the intensely loving God she had experienced. One hour of this and she was tired and ready to say *sext* at midday.

By that time, Alice had placed the main meal of the day on the windowsill, usually fish, bread, and ale, which Julian ate in silence by herself. A time of rest followed – sometimes even a nap, and then *none*.

When she rose from these prayers, Julian broke her silence. She sat by her window, ready for two or three hours of counselling with those who came to her. And hard conversations they often were, for the times were troubled and life was often bitter for those who came to her curtained window. Sometimes there were more pleasant conversations with her mother, or the abbess, or Alice. Thomas came for the occasional visit, though they were less and less frequent and each time he seemed more unsettled and angry. Her concern for her brother was often the text of her prayers.

After her time at the window, Julian was often tired and needed the spiritual refreshment she found in *vespers.*

Julian had a light second meal in the late afternoon or early evening, a snack really, which she usually shared with Alice at her window, and sometimes with her mother who might be visiting. Then, to bring the day to a close, *compline.*

In the monasteries and convents, *compline* was the beginning of "the great silence," which lasted through the night office, and *lauds* which followed immediately, until after *prime* in the morning.

Word of this rhythm soon spread in Norwich, along with her reputation as a counsellor. If someone came at any time other than in the late afternoon, Julian ignored their calls at her window, unless the caller sounded absolutely desperate. Then she might break her silence to help. If Alice heard the calling, she would say to the visitors, "The anchorite is at prayer. Please come back this afternoon."

Julian fully lived the life of a solitary. Silence. Prayer. Reflection. And she was determined to guard that solitude, which she came to treasure more with each passing day. But she also treasured the conversations at her window, conversations that enriched her solitude, just as her solitude enriched her interactions with the spiritually hungry folk who came every day now. More and more, she appreciated the fundamental wisdom of her anchoritic life, how her deep solitude made it possible for her to care intensely for the spiritual and material welfare of each soul who came looking to her for hope.

It took Julian more than two months to write the twenty-five chapters of her book, saying each sentence, each phrase out loud before she wrote it down. And even when she put down the pen for the last time, she knew the writing was incomplete.

There was one vision she had not written down simply because she didn't know what to make of it. It was a parable about a lord who dearly loved his servant, and an eager servant who dearly loved his lord. And the servant went running on an errand for the lord, and was so eager to please, that he fell into a ditch.

But what was that all about?

"Someday, perhaps, God will show me," she muttered to herself. But for now at least, she was done with the writings. She bundled the sheets of parchment and sent them with Alice to the abbess. Two days after that, the abbess was at her window. "My daughter," the older woman was smiling and shaking her head. "You have written well! These writings show God's power and God's love in a way I've never experienced before. May I have them read to the sisters at Carrow when we take our meals?"

Julian was dumbfounded. "Why yes, of course, Mother Abbess."

"Now that you have written these visions, what do you plan to do with your hands when you are not at prayer?"

"I haven't given it any thought." Julian paused. Then she answered with a singular lack of enthusiasm. "I suppose I could do needlework."

The abbess snorted. "You hate needlework and you're no good at it."

Julian pulled back her head from the window, pretending to be offended.

"Some anchorites have earned a few pennies copying books. If I can convince the prior in the cathedral monastery that you are a fair copyist, would you like to do that? I will show him the book of psalms you copied for the abbey."

"But I know so very little of the Latin."

"That's nonsense, Julian! You already know more Latin than most priests. Anyway, you will be copying words, not writing your own. And you will learn much of the Latin as you copy it."

Julian tried to laugh away the compliment, but she could see the abbess meant it. "I would be most pleased to do it. But if there is payment for such work, I would rather it went to Carrow. I have no need of more than the stipend you give Alice to buy food."

"As you wish. Are you happy here, child?"

"Reverend Mother Cecily, I am thirty-one years old. I am not a child. And I don't know if I am happy. But I am content."

"That is enough," said the abbess, and gathered her skirts and walked down the road to Carrow.

—

"Anchorite. I would talk with you!" The strong, young voice came through the curtain and startled Julian from her meditation.

"Who are you?" she asked. The abbess had told her never to pull back her curtain till she knew who was on the other side.

"I'm Maggie Baxter. I come from Martham. I would speak with you." She reached inside Julian's window and pulled back the curtain.

"The curtain is mine to draw or close as I will," said Julian testily. "What do you wish to speak about."

"My husband. William is his name. Gibberish. That's what he's talkin'. It's all gibberish."

"What kind of gibberish?"

"He's a carpenter. We've been married one year and still wait for a child. Two weeks ago he went with other carpenters to the forest to chop wood for his craft. It's two days walkin' out, and four days walkin' back carryin' the wood because the forest in these parts is all owned by the monastery. He's never in good spirits when he gets back and I don't blame him. But this time he come back spoutin' nonsense."

Julian waited. She didn't find herself liking this cocky youngster too much, but tried hard not to let that get in the way of a conversation.

"They was talkin' religion, those men. All the way there and all the way back, it seems. And William, he comes home sayin' that there's some new things these men are sayin'. Have you ever heard of Lollards, miss?"

"No," said Julian simply.

"Me neither. William says they follow the thinkin' of a man named Wycliffe, John Wycliffe, who's a schoolman in Oxford. He's sayin' that if a priest or a monk is livin' crooked, like keepin' a woman or like that, then you don't have to pay them their tithe. They got no right to ask for your money."

"Do you believe that?"

"I don't know what I believe. That's why I come here so's you could set me right, miss."

"But what do you think?"

"Well, look, if folks stopped payin' their tithe every time one of them priests was gettin' a little nooky on the side, there wouldn't be much money goin' their way, now would there? So it's no good askin' the priests. You know what they'd tell you."

"So then you know who to ask."

"Who?"

"God. You ask God what's the right thing to do."

"You mean me? I should start prayin' right to God as if I'm a priest or somethin'? I don't know no Latin."

"God hears your prayer just as surely as God hears the prayers of a bishop."

"Well, now, that's another thing those men was saying. Anybody can pray. Just like that. All my life I've been thinkin' it's us folks who pay the priests and the priests do the proper prayin', 'septin' for the things they give us to say in church. You know, like the *Ave Maria* and the *Pater Noster*. And now you and William tell me I can do the prayin' for myself. I wouldn't know how to do it."

"God understands English."

"Where did you come up with that, now?"

"Well, I pray to God and I don't speak Latin. God speaks to me in English."

"Well, ain't that somethin'! And how will I know if it's God that's talkin' back to me and not the devil?"

"If your prayer is real – if you deeply and truly mean every word you say, and if you believe God is hearing your prayer, then you'll know, Maggie."

"You're sure of that now?"

"I'm sure."

"Somethin' else William was sayin'. He says this John Wycliffe and his schoolmen are fixin' to write the Bible in the English tongue. What do you think of that?"

"It would be a fine thing if more people could hear the gospels in their own language. I don't think there is anything in the teaching of the church that says God's word must only be written in Latin."

Maggie began rummaging around in her scrip. "Well, I gotta pop along. I guess I should give you some money for takin' your time."

"I don't need your money. But I do need your prayers. Will you pray for me too?"

"Me? Pray for you? Now that's somethin'. Things keep changin' all the time," said Maggie, shaking her head. "All the time." She began to leave, then said, "Next time I come to Norwich, I'll come see you again."

"I'd like that," said Julian. "But let *me* decide whether to open the curtain."

As she watched the woman go, Julian felt uneasy about the conversation. Was she saying things that would anger the priests – the bishop? Of course anyone could pray to God anytime in any language. Of course there was no reason the Bible should not be written in English. This was the teaching of the Church. But in reality, few people did their own praying, and most people, even many of the priests, believed that God understood only Latin. Ordinary, unlettered folk, like Maggie and the apprentices to the trades, like the villeins who tilled the land, believed that only the prayer of priests or holy people reached God. Common folks could pray, but only in the snippets of memorized Latin given to them by the priests. Never in words of their own.

Julian raised the question with the abbess when she came to

the window a few days later. "I believe what Holy Church teaches," Julian sighed. "But that isn't always what the priests tell the people, and it isn't always the way the church acts."

"That is true, Julian," the abbess responded. "We pray for peace and love and community, but the priests and bishops and popes talk of war, of anger, and privilege. I don't understand it either. I've stopped trying. But I do believe God weeps for us all. I have stopped trying to understand the church and try only to hear the voice of God."

The older woman saw the look of dejection on Julian's face. "There is hope. There is beauty. There is truth, Julian. You have written about it in your book. We have only begun to read it to the nuns at mealtimes, but already I can see a glow on some faces that was not there before. It's the first time we have had a book in English to read at mealtimes – the first time they've heard something they really understand. I've not told them where the book came from, although Sister Joan knows. She will not tell them. It is better this way, because some of your teachings will be misunderstood and they will find their way to the ears of priests. They can rail against me all they wish. I do not answer to the bishop. But they could hurt you, Julian."

"You are very good to me, Reverend Mother. Why?"

"Because I have come to love you as a daughter, and because you are doing the things I dreamed of doing when I was younger. By the way, I have something for you."

The abbess rose and went to the door. "Take that bundle into the maid's room," she called. A young man approached Alice's door with a heavy-looking bundle. "Set it on the bench," said the abbess, who had followed the man into Alice's room. "You may go back to Carrow and resume your work. Thank you."

"Drat these knots," the abbess complained. "They tie them so tight, my sore old fingers can't undo them."

"Let me do it," said Alice, excited as a child receiving a gift. She quickly ripped off the rough cord that held the linen wrapping around the parcel. "It's a book, ma'am!" Alice was wide-eyed. "I ain't never seen a book this big! And a whole pile of parchment."

"That's right, Alice," the abbess smiled. "And Julian is going to copy that big book onto that parchment. We have to give her something to keep her out of trouble. Idle hands are the devil's playground, they say. The book is Matthew's gospel, Alice. It's part of the Bible. Julian copied Mark's gospel when she was at Carrow. I didn't think that was wise at the time, but when I showed her work to the prior, he said it was very well done. So now he wants Julian to copy some more. When she's done this one, I'll bring her Luke's gospel, then John, and who knows – we may get her all the way through the Bible if she lives long enough."

"Ma'am," said Alice through the window into Julian's room, "if I stood near the window while you was readin' the words while you write them, I could hear what the book says. I ain't much smart, but I could learn somethin'."

"Good idea, Alice," said the abbess. "Besides, the *Ancrene Wesse* says that anchorites are responsible for their maid's spiritual education. But the words here are in the Latin tongue, Alice. Julian knows some Latin, but she will learn much more, especially if she tells you in English what the Latin words are saying. What do you think of that, Julian?"

"You are a slave-driver, Mother Abbess," Julian laughed. "Alice, you and I are about to be educated, whether we want to be or not. But Mother Cecily, you will need to come by every day or so to explain the Latin words I don't understand."

"I always enjoy coming to visit you two. Now I'll have a good excuse. I can't come every day, but I'll come as often as I can." She reached through the window from Alice's room and touched Julian's hand, and gave Alice a peck on the cheek. Then she was gone.

So began the slow, word-by-word copying, and the laboured translation for Alice. Julian made it very clear that this period was part of her time of silence. She said the words out loud in Latin, then wrote them painstakingly on the parchment. Then she offered an English rendering for Alice, though she soon realized this exercise helped her own understanding as well. If Alice had questions or comments, she was to keep them to herself till they shared their evening meal together. Alice found it hard to contain herself sometimes. The morning's reading bounced around in her mind till she almost pounced on Julian when she placed the evening meal on the window ledge.

Thomas came by one afternoon. He was a priest now, serving a parish just outside of Norwich. But he was cold and distant and seemed in a hurry to get the visit done – as if he had come more out of duty than out of pleasure. To make conversation, Julian told him about the gospel she was copying, and how she was translating it for Alice.

"There's too much of that going on!" Thomas burst out suddenly. "God's holy book should not be in the hands of lay people, especially women. You should spend more time in prayer and less time with books. And ask God's help to live your proper station in life. Holy Church has too many enemies about. My sister should not be one of them."

"I am doing this for the prior at the cathedral, Thomas!" she protested.

"That may be so!" Thomas was almost shouting now. "But the prior is not always as careful as he should be to guard the sanctity and privileges of Holy Church!" Then he stood up abruptly and left. Julian ached for Thomas, for the pain and confusion she could see in his dark and tired eyes.

Copying the Gospel of Matthew and translating it for Alice added a good and wholesome aspect to the rhythm of their lives, Julian thought. Sometimes the rhythm was punctuated by small surprises, such as the day Alice came in, with bleeding scratches up and down her arms. She was carrying a cat. "He's been hangin' around the churchyard for days now. I give him some bits of food 'cause he was starvin' thin. He scratched me real good when I picked him up. Just as stupid as people, he is. Scratches and bites those tryin' to help him. Can we keep him around to help catch the mice? There was rats runnin' around here yesterday."

"Why not?" said Julian. "The *Ancrene Wisse* says an anchorite can have a cat. Not a cow, Alice, because the stiff old man who wrote that book thinks it'll get into the neighbour's yard and make trouble. But a cat is fine."

There was no name for the cat at first. But as it began to trust Julian and Alice, as its fur became sleek from the tidbits Alice fed him, it became part of their little family. Sometimes, when Julian was hard at her copying, the cat would lie on her lap and purr. And if the weather was cold, Julian would warm her hands in its fur. Besides, it made the anchorhold somewhat less lonely. "He's a joy to me," said Julian one day. And so "Joy" became the animal's name.

Some mornings Maud joined Julian and Alice in their morning copying session. She sat silently at the window with Alice, then became so intrigued by what she heard, she returned that night for the conversation. And Maud kept coming back, even though she complained of her stiffening limbs, and how hard it was to walk the distance from Carrow to Saint Julian's twice each day.

"It's wonderfully interesting and I'm learning so much," Maud said one evening. "But I can't do it anymore. My old legs are just too tired." Suddenly, Julian noticed how old and thin her mother looked.

When Maud hadn't visited for a whole week, Julian sent Alice to find out why. She came back looking concerned. "Your mama was lookin' awful old, ma'am. And she's gettin' skinny. I asked Sister Joan what was happenin' with her, but she don't know neither. She says she thinks maybe your mama is gettin' ready to die."

That possibility hit Julian like a bolt out of the blue. The reality of her enclosure overcame her in a way it had never done before. "My mother is dying and I can't even go to see her!" She cried angrily for several minutes, then shouted at Alice. "I don't care about this anchorhold and copying all those stupid Latin words. I am going to see my mother. She is not going to die alone!"

"Ma'am, please." Alice opened the door and went into the anchorhold with Julian. She shut the door behind her. "Ma'am, don't do something stupid when you've got your arse in your armpits. Sit down for a while. Your mama's not going to die right away."

Julian sat in silence for a long while, wrestling with the conflict in her soul – her need to be with her mother, her commitment to the anchorhold. Then she went to her kneeler and Alice returned to her room. Alice knew without asking that Julian was taking her conflict to God in prayer.

Several hours later, Julian pulled the curtain back on the window into Alice's room. "Did God tell you what to do?" Alice wondered.

"No. But I did hear God saying to me that I was to trust, and that all will be well."

"Well, maybe God can't figure it out neither, but I ain't goin' to sit here with my finger up my nose waitin'. I'm goin' back to Carrow and talk to Sister Joan and maybe we can figure a way that won't have you breakin' promises and throwin' your life out the window. Now you get yourself onto your knees some more and you pray about your mama and about yourself. And promise me you won't do nothin' stupid till I get back."

Julian did as she was told. Whenever she became weak, Alice seemed to rise in strength and take charge. Before she left, Alice brought in a large cup of brew made from Saint John's Wort. "Your favourite drink, ma'am. It tastes so vile, it must be doin' some good." Then Alice was out the door, closing it firmly behind her. Julian heard the bolt slide. Unless she wanted to climb through the small window into the alcove, Julian was locked inside.

Two hours later, Alice was back. "Sister Joan went in and talked to the abbess, and we've got the whole thing figured out. They's gonna hitch up a horse and wagon, and they's puttin' a whole bunch of straw mattresses in the wagon, and they're gonna load your mama into it, and bring her here."

"But there's no room here, Alice! And even if there was, I'm not allowed to have anyone in the anchorhold here with me. You know that."

"We got that figured too, ma'am. Your mama's gonna sleep in my bed, and I'm gonna to sleep in the church. The abbess said she was goin' to talk to the priest and tell him there better not be any funny stuff when I'm there in the church alone." Alice began giggling.

"What are you laughing at?"

"Mother Abbess telling that priest to keep his hands off me. He's a little shrivelled up old man who wouldn't know what to do if I ran around starkers."

Alice laughed again, then took a deep breath. "If you need me for anything, you can just holler through the squint. You can talk to your mama through the window, and I can take care of her. Sister Joan says she's going to give me a whole bag of that Wort stuff, but I figure your mama's hurtin' enough, we don't need to make her drink that slop."

"Alice, you are wonderful!" Julian reached through the window and took her maid's hand, marvelling at how much this woman had grown in the time they had been together.

Maud arrived the next day, not lying on the mattress of straw as Alice had planned, but sitting on the seat beside the driver. "This is nonsense, Julian," Maud grumped after she had walked slowly and painfully into Alice's room in the anchorhold. "You've got important things to do, and you have no need to be looking after an old crone." With the help of Alice, she lowered herself slowly and painfully onto a small stool. "I wouldn't be here if Alice and Sister Joan and even the abbess hadn't been standing there, glaring at me, commanding me to go. It's nonsense, Julian. You have better things to do."

"And I love you too, Mama." Julian smiled through her tears.

"Anyways, we need someone else in here," said Alice, trying to look very stern. "Julian spends most of her time prayin' so it'll be real nice to have someone here to talk to. And I've heard everything Julian has to say twenty times."

Alice carried the straw mattresses from the wagon, then removed hers into the church. "You'll be living in the lap of luxury, missus. Two fat mattresses to lie on. They only give them nuns at Carrow one skinny little one. And you'll have both me and Julian to look after you."

"I am blessed with two wonderful daughters." Maud spoke very softly. "I thank God for my Alice and my Julian every day."

Julian found she got very little copying done during the next few weeks, but she quickly set aside her small pangs of guilt and frustration over that. Julian had dedicated herself to the work of God when she entered the anchorhold, her *opus Dei*. For now, part of that work, the copying and study of the gospels, needed to be set aside. For now, her *opus Dei* was to be with her mother in her dying.

So Julian broke her silence for about an hour late each morning and she and Maud talked through the window. They talked about the past, about their family. There was soft laughter sometimes, and occasional tears. Sister Joan had sent word to Thomas and he came one afternoon looking very concerned. The mantle of his priesthood hung uncomfortably from his slight frame and narrow shoulders. He still looked angry and distracted.

"Have you asked the priest to come and hear your confession and give you the Holy Eucharist?" he asked. "Do you want me to hear your confession?"

"All in good time, son," said Maud. "I'm not dead yet."

Thomas gave Julian an annoyed glance. "We never know the hour of our dying, Mother."

"No. But I will do all that is necessary before I die. Your sister will see to that."

"Then, sister," Thomas commanded, "see to it that Mother has proper spiritual care from her priest." Thomas bent over, gave his mother a perfunctory kiss and left. Alice had gone to the market. Mother and daughter sat together for a while in silence – Julian leaning through the window, Maud lying on her straw mattress, wondering about the anger in her son. And wondering about her death.

In spite of her uneasy relationship with God, Maud was absolutely certain there was life after death. It was not the dying that frightened her. It was the prospect of many years in purgatory before heaven would open to her. She knew, because that's what she had been taught, that she could spend an eternity in hell if she died in a state of sin – if she had not received the last rites of the church.

Thinking about that got Maud agitated and angry. "There was no priest to bless my husband and my children. Most of the priests were dead from the plague. Is your father writhing in hell's agony because there was no priest for him when I dragged him out to be thrown with other corpses into a pit, Julian?" It was more of a challenge than a question.

"Mama, no. The priests are there to help us – to lead our souls to God. The sacraments they offer us feed us with the love of Christ. But God reaches toward our souls in many ways and our souls reach out to God."

"Are your father and our children in hell because there was no one to hear their confession?" Maud's eyes brightened in anger. "If that's where they are, I want to go there too."

"I don't think they are in hell, Mama. The sacraments of the church, especially the Mass, are a good way and a holy way, but they are not the only way. I have heard God say to me, 'Suddenly you will be taken from all your pain, from all your sickness, from all your distress, and from all your woe. And you shall come up to me, and my love will be your reward. And then you will be filled with love and joy.' No more pain, Mama. No more struggle, no more anxiety. That was God's gift to Papa and to everyone."

"Well, how do I know there is anything after death. The worms eat our bodies, we return to the soil and that's the end of it."

"Mama, one of the visions God sent to me, showed me a horrifying sight – of a corpse all bloated and out of shape and stinking. But then, suddenly, out of this body sprang a beautiful creature, a little child fully formed, nimble and lively. There was nothing evil, or odd, or foul about this child. By that child I understood God to mean a soul. When Papa died, his soul was newborn and rose up to God, like that new child in the vision."

Julian felt the tears in her own eyes, and saw the tears in her mother's.

"I want to believe that so much, Julian," said Maud. "But I still have this knot of pain deep inside me, which I have tried and tried to pray away. The pain comes from my anger at God. Why doesn't God take away that pain?"

Julian summoned all her strength, all her wisdom from reading and counselling, to find the right words for her mother. She took a deep breath to compose her thoughts. Then she said, carefully measuring every word, "God does not take the pain away from us, Mama. God takes *us* away from the pain. That is why death is a gift – even the foul deaths of those we loved so dearly and who died so horribly."

It was an impulse, but a strong one. Julian broke her own rule. She went through the door into Alice's room and felt only slightly guilty about it. She sat with her mother through the night, stroking her hand when Maud's sleep became agitated. She sat there, praying perhaps, although there were no words on her lips or even in her mind. It was a time of holiness, of mystery, of beauty, of joy, of hope. Never had she felt so close to her mother, never felt such a deep sense of love for her, never felt so closely held and nurtured in the arms of Jesus.

When the first light of dawn shone through the edge of the oiled-linen window, Maud opened her eyes wide, looked Julian full in the face, smiled, and nodded slightly.

Then she died.

Julian felt no need to cry, no need to pray. She sat there in the slow light of morning, sensing the presence of her mother with her in the little room. Then, as if to free her mother's spirit from the confines of the cell, she opened the door and felt the morning sun fall full upon her. "Goodbye, Mama. Papa and your children and your grandchildren are waiting for you. They love you and God loves you."

Alice came in a few moments later. Julian put an arm around her and the two women stood before the body that now seemed so tiny and so frail. Alice cried softly for a while, then looked at Julian. "You've been awake all night, haven't you? Go to bed, Julian, and sleep. I'll go talk to Sister Joan and we'll figure out what needs to be done."

Julian lay on her mat and for a moment wondered why she had no tears now, why she felt no grief at her mother's death. Loneliness, yes. Gratitude, yes. But not grief.

And then she slept.

1381

For the almighty truth of the Trinity
is our Father,
who made us and keeps us.
And the deep wisdom of the Trinity
is our Mother,
in whom we are all enclosed.
And the high goodness of the Trinity
is our Lord Jesus.
We are enclosed in him
and he in us.

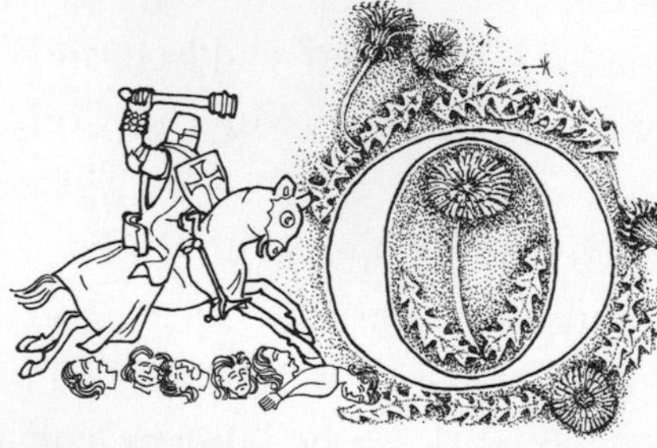

On a warm, sunny afternoon in late May, Alice brought a bunch of blood-red roses in from the garden. Julian touched and smelled them, then noticed that Alice seemed troubled. She handed Julian her trencher of cabbage and cornmeal, and a small jug of ale.

"You're very quiet today, Alice," Julian commented.

"Strange things was bein' said by the women at the well when I was gettin' water today, ma'am."

Julian waited. She knew Alice would tell her as soon as she found the words.

"A hedge priest has been preachin' in the towns around Norwich."

"Why is that strange, Alice? There are always wandering priests about, saying strange things. Is this one different?"

"Yes, ma'am. His name is John Ball and he come north from Colchester. He is preachin' that villeins who work the land and shopkeepers are the equal of the nobles and lords and bishops. And some are saying that his preachin' is true. They say he has a little rhyme:

'When Adam delved and Eva span,
Who was then the gentleman?'

They say in the market that the bishop's men will chop him down soon enough."

"Is he coming to Norwich?"

Julian's question was answered the next afternoon when a man knocked on Alice's door. "I am looking for the anchorite that I may have her counsel," a male voice called.

When Alice opened her door, she was greeted by a young priest wearing a large, brown habit of coarse wool fastened with a cord, a rosary, and an unkempt beard. He was tall and large boned, with a ring of straggly hair around his priestly tonsure. Below his imposing nose was a large firm mouth that could light up easily into a warm smile. Alice could see he was one of the wandering priests, the "hedge priests" as ordinary folks called them, or *sacerdos vagans* as they were named by the church hierarchy.

Alice led the priest to the anteroom of Julian's cell. "The anchorite is at prayer, Father. She will speak with you when she is ready. Can you wait a short while?"

"Yes, madam," said the priest, bowing slightly. Alice jumped, almost as if she had been attacked.

"I'm sorry, madam," said the priest. "Did I offend you?"

"No sir. No. But I am a maidservant. I should not be called madam, as if I were a lady."

"Most certainly you should," said the priest. "You are the equal of any lady. You deserve to be addressed with respect. All of God's people deserve to be treated with respect."

"Could you be John Ball?" asked Alice incredulously. "I have heard it said you come from heaven!"

"Aye! That is my name. But I did not come from heaven, merely from Essex. It seems my reputation precedes me. But I am not the only one who has a reputation. Your mistress, Mother Julian, is spoken of with respect in many places, because it is said she gives wise and gentle counsel. That is why I have come to see her. I am in need of her wisdom."

Alice was still wide-eyed. "It is said in the market that the bishop's men will come and chop you down like a weed in the garden."

"No doubt. That is why I never tarry long in one place. The Archbishop of Canterbury commanded me to be silent, and people are forbidden to listen to my words. But words of truth cannot be stifled any more than the sun can be commanded not to shine."

"Is it true you say that villeins and shopkeepers are the equal of lords and nobles?"

"Aye! And so they are."

"But the priests and bishops say otherwise!"

"That they do. But that is not the best teaching of the church. The best teachers of Holy Church, like Saint Paul, have long said that all are equal in the sight of God, that in Christ there is neither Jew nor Gentile, male nor female, slave nor freeborn."

Neither Alice nor Father John had noticed that the curtain into Julian's cell had been opened silently and she was sitting at her window, smiling.

"You are a dangerous man, John Ball," said Julian quietly. Alice quickly retreated to her room. "And I am pleased and honoured to make your acquaintance. Alice, the woman you were just speaking with, tells me you are the talk of the marketplace."

"Indeed, and for that reason I must move along very soon. The talk of the market does not take long to reach the ears of the earl or the bishop."

"Then what do you need of me, Father John."

"Reassurance. There is trouble in the land. The king has levied a head tax, four pence on the head of every man, woman, and child, and this to support the king's quarrel with France. The people are groaning under the load of it, the poor more than the wealthy. There have been crop failures and pestilence that killed the cattle, and yet the tax collectors show no mercy. Already there have been villeins who have used their pitchforks on the tax collectors. In the face of desperation, people often do not consider the consequences. What is now a spark could easily become a flame, and then we will all be burned by it."

Julian found herself warming to this bright-eyed prophet. "Are you not fanning that spark by your preaching?"

"Aye. Which is why I have come to you. Am I speaking truth?"

"Tell me what you are speaking."

"I have heard tell of preaching across the sea in Flanders. Jan van Ruysbroeck has been speaking against 'a false vacancy,' those who ignore the cries of the people going up to God. The lords and bishops and abbots refuse to hear the cries of the villeins, and of the poor in the cities. But God hears their cries, just as God heard the cries of the Hebrew slaves in Egypt. Those who refuse to hear the cries of the slaves are evil."

"Ah, but Father John, we have no slaves in England!" Ball did not miss the sarcasm in her voice.

"It is true, Mother Julian. We have no slaves. We have villeins who have at least one freedom – they are free to die without the permission of their lords. Beyond that, they have nothing to hope for except heaven, and the church has taken even that away, claiming heaven is only there for those who buy the prayers of the clergy."

The priest stood up and faced out to the street. His voice began to rise. "God is with the villeins of England as God was with the slaves in Egypt, and I have been going about from town to town with the cry of Moses. 'Let my people go!'" Julian could see his strong shoulders heave in anger, then sag in grief. Father John turned and sat down. Julian thought she saw tears in his eyes. "Or do you not believe, Mother Julian, that these serfs are loved..." his voice broke and he struggled to control his emotions. "Are they loved by God?"

"Oh, indeed. And more than that." Julian did not raise her voice, but it trembled with intensity and passion. "It is in the nature of the Trinity that God offered us the most gracious gift of all imagining – our precious Lord Jesus. He came to us as a human being, not as a lord or a lady, not as a bishop or a priest, but of the same substance as every one of us, the same substance as the poorest, most miserable villein. This is the teaching of Holy Church, is it not?"

The priest nodded.

"Our human nature is joined to God through Christ. We are made of the same holy stuff God is made of. Just as we put clothes on our bodies, and our flesh clothes our skin, and bones in our flesh and our heart deep inside, so we are Father John, you and I, and the villein scratching the hard earth, and the lords and the bishops, clothed in the goodness of God." The priest was looking at Julian with an intensity she had not seen before. "We are soul and body, clad in the endless love of God," she plunged on breathlessly. "This is the teaching of the Trinity. This is the best teaching of Holy Church, even though that teaching is seldom heard in these troubled times."

Julian was finding it hard to focus her mind on their topic of discussion. She found her eyes drawn to the intensity of his. In this rough priest she sensed a kindred soul – a sense of unity with a man she had never experienced before.

"Aye, Mother." The priest now spoke with ringing passion but barely above a whisper. "The prophets of old cried out against those who grind the faces of the poor, who sell the righteous for a pair of sandals, and who neglect the alien, the orphan, and the widow. So taught Saint Francis and those who follow him rightly." Suddenly he was almost shouting. "But things cannot go well in England, nor shall they ever, till all the wealth of this nation is held in common, until our church sees the naked and wounded Christ walking the dusty roads of England. Till there is no longer bond nor free, priest nor parishioner, but all of us are equal. Until the church is again as it was in the time of the apostles, as it is told in Holy Scripture, when all things were held in common. There were no rich and there were no poor in the first days of Holy Church. And it is to that teaching that we must return." Then his voice broke slightly. "Or do I speak falsely?"

Father John spoke with such intensity it made Julian shiver. Even through the window, she could smell the sweat of his passion and fear. She measured her words in reply. "Whether you speak true or false is not for me to judge. I only know what I have been shown. And I have been shown a most courteous Lord who looks with love and joy on all creation. The least as well as the greatest. That is what I believe Holy Church teaches, that God loved the world dearly and sent the Lord Jesus so that all – *all* who believed might be saved." Julian was silent for a long while and in the silence their eyes met and said more than their words. Finally Julian whispered. "But that is not always what we hear in the pulpits. Nevertheless it is the teaching of the church. That is what I declare to those who come to my window for counsel, and that is what you say you preach."

"Then perhaps we are on the same mission, Mother Julian."

"Yes." Again there was silence between them. Finally Julian turned to him, smiling slightly, though there were tears in her eyes. "We have the same vocation, Father John, though we live it differently. I am called by God to pray here in my solitude, and give hope and counsel to those who come to my window. You are called to declare that teaching in the markets – to shout it from the housetops."

Julian read the passion and the fear in her new friend's face. His hands trembled slightly. "I shall pray for you, Father John. The world does not deal kindly with those who want to turn it upside down. You will be 'despised and rejected,' as our Lord was. And you may well pay for your passion with your life. Christ does not promise us that life will be sweet and easy. But Christ does promise to be with us, through all that we have to bear. Go in peace, brother. In the long vision of God, all shall be well. Pray for me as I will pray most earnestly for you."

She held her hand out through the window to this strong, vulnerable man as he stood up to leave. Her fingers trembled, as did his. As the two hands gently touched, both knew themselves to share with the other the work of God. Julian the contemplative. John Ball the prophet.

"If I am still alive to do so, I will come and see you again."

"Yes."

Father John crossed himself and left. Julian also crossed herself, pulled the curtain across the window, and told Alice she was not to be disturbed.

Her heart full of fear and dread, Mother Julian knelt to pray.

—

Bishop Henry's man came two days later. "I require an audience with the anchorite," he said briskly to Alice. "Immediately!"

Julian heard inside her cell. She responded through the closed curtain when she heard him step into the anteroom. "I am the anchorite here at Saint Julian's. May I know who you are and what your pleasure may be?"

"I am Reginald, a priest in the service of Bishop Henry. Do you not open your curtain to your betters?"

"I have been instructed to open my curtain only to those who wish me well and mean no harm."

Father Reginald was clearly angry at her response. "Did you have a traitor visit your cell recently, a false priest by the name of John Ball?"

"I do not ask of anyone whether they be true or false, nor what station they have in life. As best I can, I assure them of the goodness of God, and then I pray for them. But yes, there was a man named John Ball who came to see me."

"And what was your conversation?"

"We spoke of the Holy Trinity, and of God's loving gifts."

"Did he speak sedition?"

"He said nothing to me that is not taught by Holy Church."

"What did he want of you?"

"He asked for my prayers."

"Well, you are not to pray for him. He is a false priest and a traitor."

"My calling is to pray for *all* who ask. That was the instruction given by Bishop Henry at the time of my enclosure. I will pray for John Ball, and I will pray for you, if you wish."

"I have no need of your prayers, woman." Julian could hear the anger, even if she could not see Father Reginald's flushed face. "Where did he go when he left here?"

"We did not speak of that. I have no knowledge of his work or of his whereabouts."

"Beware of whom you speak to, woman. There is trouble brewing and you had best keep your nose clear of it." He turned and left.

Julian waited till she was sure he had gone. Then she went to her other window. "Alice?"

"Yes, ma'am?"

"What are they saying in the market? What is happening in the town?"

"I don't know, ma'am. But I see men standin' around gabbin'. Women too. And sometimes they start to shoutin'. I heard say there was fightin' in Essex, and some priests have had their heads chopped off, and there have been murders and much quarrelin'. And y'can't buy hardly nothin' in the market. Folks are stayin' at home, and we're not goin' to have much to eat 'ceptin' bread and gruel, 'cause there ain't no fish nor meat nor nothin' much."

Rumours flew everywhere the next few weeks. No one was sure of anything except that there was great trouble in the land. Small gangs and large masses of villeins, joined by the crafters of the middle class, mixed with some clergy and a few lesser nobles, were looting and burning and raping and killing. Often they were joined by those who had no cause except their own – to settle old grudges or to justify their pillage of the wealthy. It was mostly the gentry and the monasteries that bore the brunt of their anger. And the bishops.

"They have murdered the archbishop of Canterbury," moaned Mother Abbess. "And they will come and murder us and burn us too, I'm sure."

"Why?" wondered Julian. "You have no great wealth or power."

"Far more than you know, my child. Carrow Abbey owns lands on which we have villeins in servitude. Not as much land as the cathedral priory, to be sure, or the bishop or the Earl of Norfolk. But some of our villeins have joined the revolt. And they have good reason, Julian. We have not treated them well."

Julian noticed that Mother Abbess seemed suddenly very old and frail. "Where can you go, Mother Cecily, so that you will be safe? Do you want to stay with me here, in my cell?"

"If I stayed here, *you* would not be safe. You are safe, Julian, only because you have no money and no power, and everyone in the town knows that. There is nothing to be gained by ransacking your poor cell. No, I will go back to the abbey."

"Have you heard anything of a priest named John Ball, Mother?"

The old woman looked surprised. "Do you know the man?"

"He came by my cell some weeks ago and begged me for my prayers. I think he is a man of vision – a man of God. He holds the teaching of Holy Church that all of us are made in God's image, and if that is so, then no one should be lord over any other."

"That is what he preaches, certainly. I am told he says that since all of us are descendants of Adam and Eve, why should some be masters and others do their bidding? He is preaching openly around London and the crowds flock to hear him. He stirs up much mischief."

"Does he not speak true?"

Mother Abbess was silent, thinking. Then she shook her head and sighed. "Yes. Yes, I think so. My head tells me he is a trouble-maker and the ruin of all God's work through Holy Church. My heart knows he speaks the gospel – that what we do to the least of God's family, we do to God."

The two women sat in silence for a while, both wanting to speak words of encouragement, but neither of them finding any. "I am very tired, Julian. I will go back to the abbey and I will pray that whatever happens be God's will."

"Amen," said Julian as she reached through the window for the old woman's hand and kissed it.

Alice returned running from the market only minutes after she had left. She raced inside her room and bolted the door. "Ma'am! Ma'am! Terrible stuff is happenin' all over town. The place is full of men from everywhere, and they have clubs and sticks and sometimes spears and swords, and they're yellin' that they're gonna to kill all the monks and all the gentry and they say they're even gonna to kill the bishop. And there's fires burning somewhere 'cause the whole sky is dark with smoke. I'm awful scared, ma'am!"

"Of course," said Julian. "So am I. There was no priest in St. Julian's this morning. For the first time since I came into this anchorhold, I was not able to hear mass. Every morning I have meditated on the body and blood of Christ, and now..." Julian's lips moved as if to say more and confusion spread across her face.

"What are we gonna do? I'm scared!"

"Well. Let me think." Julian walked around her cell, whispering the prayer, "Lord, help me do the right thing." Then suddenly she turned back to Alice. "There is something we must do now, Alice. We must both pray."

"You can pray, ma'am. God don't listen to people like me."

"That's not true, Alice. God listens to you just as much as God listens to me."

"Ma'am! You're a holy woman. Everybody in the market says you are holy and wise, and that folks get good stuff told to 'em when they come to see you. That's why they've started callin' you Mother Julian. You should hear the nice things they say about you. So *you* pray..."

"Alice! God loves you, just as much as anyone else. And when you pray, God pays as close attention as when I pray or anyone else who prays. A lot of the shouting and anger you hear out there is about greed and lust and power, but some of the people – do you remember Father John Ball who came to see us? Some people like him are fighting just because they are so sure God loves everyone the same, and so they should be treated the same. John Ball and others are willing to die for it."

"But, ma'am. I ain't nothing but a foundling and a whore."

"Alice!" Julian barked so loudly she surprised even herself. "The world is burning around us, and you and I need to do something right now. You don't have to believe God hears your prayers when all this is over. But for now, you've got to believe it. God hears your prayers and honours the love you have in year heart. I have never given you a flat order before, but I am ordering you right now, Alice. Until this trouble is over, you are to think of yourself as being just as precious to God as anyone else in the world. And you are to pray as if God hears you. Do you understand?"

"Yes, ma'am."

"You and I are going to pray, like we've never prayed before. All we're going to say is, 'Thy will be done, Lord.' Just those words. Over and over. But in-between time, we're going to think of all the people we know, the ones we love and the ones we hate. We're going to say their names out loud, and we're going to think of all the people we don't know and we're going to hold them in our hearts, and then say, 'Thy will be done, Lord.' And we will fast, Alice, partly because there isn't much to eat here anyway, and partly because it will help us concentrate on our prayers. Don't look so horrified. We'll survive. We will drink what ale we have, and then we will drink water, and we'll have a little barley gruel each day. But other than that, we will not eat. And Alice…"

"Yes, ma'am?"

"This is probably the most important thing you and I have ever done in our lives."

Occasionally the two women heard noises in the street, and once there was clearly a group of men arguing in Saint Julian's Church. For a week they prayed, though sometimes they slept in sheer exhaustion. Alice didn't protest even once, though she looked drawn and haggard.

Joy, the cat, moved back and forth through the window, rubbing up against Alice and Julian, mewing hungrily. Eventually, it gave up and left the anchorhold entirely to search for food elsewhere.

Then one day they heard a priest singing mass. It was a most welcome sound, a sound Julian had desperately missed since the beginning of the troubles. She fairly jumped across the room to pull back the curtain from the squint. She stood and let the Eucharistic words wash her troubled soul.

Only when the mass was over did she notice that the priest was not someone she recognized. She called to him. "Are the troubles over?"

"Things are quiet," said the priest. "But our troubles remain."

"Has something happened to Father Gerard who was priest here?"

"He is dead. They say he marched with the rebels and was cut down by Bishop Despenser's men. The Abbess of Carrow will appoint a new priest in due time." Then he turned and was gone.

Julian stood there before the squint, indecision racing through her mind. "Dear Lord, help me do the right thing," she prayed silently. "Thy will be done," she whispered as she sank down onto her kneeler, and stayed there listening for guidance.

"Alice," Julian called as she stood up, her knees protesting after all the hours she had been there. "It is time to break our fast"

"Are the troubles over, ma'am?"

"I don't know. I want you to go and find out. Have something to eat. But eat slowly or your stomach will send it all back up. Whatever you have – eat something. And give some to me, but only if there is enough. You need to have some strength to find out what has happened and to get us some food."

After some barley gruel and a little bread, Alice returned to the window. "Where do you want me to go, ma'am?"

"Just look around here a little. If it seems safe, go to Carrow Abbey. Don't go to the marketplace."

Alice came back two hours later. Julian did not like the story of horror and fear Alice told with her swollen eyes. She began to weep as she lifted a small loaf of bread and some vegetables from her bag. "Mother Abbess is dead," she wailed. "Sister Joan says she died peaceful in the chapel, all by herself. They haven't had a buryin' yet because of all the troubles. A bunch of men came to Carrow and they made the nuns give them all the papers and books and stuff. Then they burned it all, and they burned part of the abbey. 'Septin' your book. Mother Abbess had it hidden in her apartment."

"Was anyone hurt?"

"No! Well, yes!"

"Alice, what happened?"

"Nobody at the abbey got hurt, as far as I can figure. But walkin' back here, I ran into one of the men that sells stuff at the market, and he told me there'd been a whole bunch of fighting in the town, and the bishop got an army and chopped some people up with swords and hung some others. And they even killed the little whoremonger!" Alice wailed more loudly than ever.

"You did care about him, didn't you, Alice," Julian suggested gently.

"I never knowed that until I started prayin' for him. When I was prayin' I got to thinkin' maybe I could talk to him a little sometime, so he wouldn't be so scared of me. He was a whinin' little snot, but he didn't know he was doin' anythin' wrong. He was stuck bein' a whoremonger 'cause he was such a little bastard, and he couldn't do no hard work and he didn't have no trade. He was just tryin' to stay alive. So now I won't never have the chance to tell him he wasn't so terrible bad."

"Maybe he knows that now, Alice. Maybe Jesus told him that when he got into heaven."

"Heaven? God don't allow no sweaty, flap-eared whoresons like that into heaven. He's frying in hell!"

"I saw you praying very hard during our vigil sometimes, Alice. I could see it on your face. Do you think God was listening?"

"Hey!" Alice stopped to think for a moment. "Yeah! God was for sure listening. I kinda knew that. How about that, eh? God listenin' to a foundling whore like me. That's a surprise! Yeah?"

"It's no more of a surprise than God listening to me, or to Bishop Henry." Julian reached through the window and touched Alice's tearful cheek. "Your small friend, Alice, had his sins forgiven even before he finished doing them. God loves us, Alice. You, me, your friend, everybody. And God is just aching to have us know that."

"So what you're sayin' ma'am, is that God don't make nothin' that's bad."

"Yes, Alice! Yes!" Even though it was a deeply tragic time for both of them, just for this moment, Julian's heart soared!

—

A strange quiet hung over the city. A few visitors came to the cell, some of them looking forlorn, stunned, some angry. Alice heard stories in the market, where gradually, day by day things got back to normal.

Bit by bit, Julian was able to piece the story together – how bands of peasants joined by struggling artisans, a few clergy, and even some lesser nobility, came close to changing the whole social structure of England. If the rebels had succeeded and lived up to their own ideals, the class structure of England, the rule of the church – everything would have been changed.

The head tax was the spark that lit the fire. It was a direct tax based on people, rather than on property. It fell heaviest on the most populated counties such as Norfolk, Suffolk, and Essex – and on the poorest people. The rich folk were supposed to help their poorer neighbours pay the tax. But of course it didn't work out that way. As people devised more and more ways to evade the tax, the tax collectors became more and more heavy handed in their imposition. Some 8,000 people in Norfolk, 600 in Norwich alone, were reputed to have evaded the tax, and the tax collectors were instructed to use any means to squeeze it out of them.

The villeins had first felt a bit of their own power in the labour shortages that followed the plagues. Now the poll tax focused that new power into active resistance and finally rebellion. It was there in their songs, too.

Now folks can't give a penny more
As you may judge by their sighs;
I think if only they found a leader,
In revolt they would arise.

Such leaders began to arise in the ferment of resentment around the poll tax – around the rising anger at the blatant immorality of far too many priests and bishops, just as the abbess had warned, and around the conspicuous overconsumption of wealth by the gentry. The governing nobles found themselves helpless and bewildered.

Many of the wandering friars spoke out against those who had lost touch with the common folk. People enjoyed the roadside and marketplace sermons of these friars, because they told stories and sang songs, and that impressed those without wealth or status. So when these hedge priests protested against the exploitation of the underclass, the discontent began to galvanize into revolt. Julian had no doubt that John Ball had done his part to fan the flames of unrest.

Wat Tyler had lead the revolt, first against Canterbury, then in London, where he was joined by John Ball. By mid-June the rebels had sacked the archbishop's palace at Lambeth and had opened two prisons at Southwark. The next day, John Ball preached at Blackheath.

"Why do the nobles and the church use us in this way?" he had shouted to the lively cheers of those assembled. "Why do they hold us in bondage? We are all descended from the same parents, Adam and Eve. If God had wanted some to be rulers and some to be in bondage, we would have been created that way right at the beginning. The rulers live in luxury and leisure. We live in penury and pain!" Soon the rallying cry became "John Ball has rung your bell!"

In East Anglia, Julian learned, the revolt attracted many villeins, but also a large number of priests and people from the governing classes. They gathered around the leadership of Geoffrey Lidster of Flemingham. The Earl of Norfolk had fled, but others of his household were captured and brought to Mousehold Heath, about a mile outside of Norwich.

The citizens of Norwich had shut the gates and raised the drawbridge, but Lidster promised them there would be no "pillage, slaughter, and arson," and so the gates were opened. Even so, there followed days of violence and burning. Most of the wealthier families had their homes sacked, though much of this was done by the rabble of the city who saw it as an opportunity to plunder. The mayor was killed as were many others, some simply because they happened to be in the wrong place at the wrong time.

Lidster made his headquarters in the castle and forced the captured knights to wait on him at table. He gave himself the title "King of the Commons." The next day, Lidster's men went into the surrounding countryside, most particularly to Carrow Abbey. There they took the deeds, the court rolls, the books in the library, anything that had writing on it, and burned them publicly in Norwich. "Away with the learning of priests!" they shouted. "Away with it!"

Then word reached them that Wat Tyler had been killed in London and that the rebellion had collapsed. Lidster retreated to a heath about a mile from North Walsham, where he prepared to make a stand.

Bishop Henry was away in Rutland when news of the rebellion reached him. Moving back toward Norwich with eight horsemen and a few archers, he suppressed several small revolts along the way and gathered more and more armed men as news of the failure of the revolt spread.

Lidster's stand was short and pitiful. Despenser ordered his archers to send a few volleys of arrows behind the row of carts the rebels had ringed around them for protection. Then he led a head-on charge at the rebels. The battle lasted only moments.

Lidster was captured in a nearby woodland. Despenser tried him immediately on the charge of taking up arms against the king's peace. There was no doubt what the verdict would be. He would be drawn, hanged, and quartered. But Despenser was not only a general and judge in the king's court, he was also bishop of Norwich, and so the fate of Lidster's soul was his responsibility. He heard the man's confession and pronounced the absolution.

Then, in what Julian could only imagine must have been a pitiful and ludicrous scene, Lidster was dragged by his feet behind a cart, toward the place of execution just outside the city near Bishop's Gate. The bishop stumbled along behind holding up Lidster's head to save it from the painful bumping on the ground. Was it kindness or was it show?

John Ball was hanged on July 15th.

Julian wept when she heard the news. John Ball had symbolized for her the best and most noble aspirations of the revolt. And she recognized the feelings she'd had for this man, feelings she'd never experienced with anyone else. She wept for a friendship that never was, and for a dream of justice and equality that was just too wild, too disorganized, too lacking in leadership, too much to expect.

"Dear Lord, how can this be?" Julian prayed. "You have told me that all shall be well, and I have believed you, but I see so much anger, hatred, murder, fear, all the things that draw us away from you. How can this be? How can you tell me that your very name is Love, when all such things come to drown us in fear?"

Bishop Despenser rode back into Norwich in triumph. The wealthier families in Norfolk County celebrated by presenting him with a magnificent reredos, a painted screen, showing the crucified Christ bleeding on the cross. The bishop had it duly installed in Saint Luke's Chapel in Norwich Cathedral.

When Julian heard about the painting many months after the revolt, she remembered her conversation with John Ball. "Our precious Lord Jesus came to us as a human being – not as a lord or as a lady, not as a bishop or as a priest – but of the same substance as every one of us; the same substance as the poorest, most miserable villein." She wondered at the painful irony of that commemorative screen that showed the agonized and painful death of Jesus, who gave his life for the poor and the lost.

Once again, Julian prayed for John Ball, for Bishop Henry, for all who had hoped and suffered. As she did so often in the confused times that swirled around her cell, she ended her prayer, "Thy will be done." But she rose from her prayers with an aching sense of futility. "Why, God, do you allow such horror to happen?"

—

Julian was delighted – and relieved – to see Sister Joan when she came to the cell about a week after the fighting was over. The nun's appearance outside the confines of the abbey meant that her status had changed. She looked tired and worried. Julian guessed at the reason. "You've taken on the responsibility at Carrow since Mother Abbess died?"

"Yes. Until a new abbess is appointed, I've been asked to act in her stead. So I have come to find out how you are."

"My body is strong, Sister Joan, but my soul is despondent. So much has been suffered in these last weeks – so much destroyed, and to what purpose? I have asked God for clarity, but it has not come."

"And I can't help you in that." Julian noticed that Sister Joan seemed much older. Her shoulders were stooped and her voice was unsteady. "I have also prayed to God about the meaning of these troubles. I've had no answer. One of the sisters at Carrow said we have to live with the question before the answer is given."

"She may be right," Julian agreed.

"Yes, she may be. Maybe we need to simply turn the question over to God. In God's good time, we will know more truth."

"I have heard it said, Sister, that the revolt of the peasants came very close to overthrowing the king and the church. The rebel's big mistake was that they trusted the king, who promised them everything they asked. They believed he would live up to his word. So they began to go back to their homes, and that's when his armed men rushed after them and killed many. Alice and I have been praying that God's will may be done in all this. Was that God's will?"

Sister Joan did not respond. Nor did Julian expect an answer. The two women sat in silence, grieving all the suffering and pain, struggling with the age-old question. Why?

"Well, Julian," sighed Sister Joan as she stood to leave, "Bishop Despenser believed he was doing God's will when he and his men crushed the revolt. The gentry all over Norfolk hold him to be a hero."

Julian shook her head sadly. "Is sin a necessary part of God's creation, Sister? I wonder sometimes, if God lets us fall more heavily and grievously than we ever did before." Julian's voice rose in frustration as her shoulders sagged. "In my prayers and meditations, God has told me many times that all shall be well, but that doesn't seem to mean that all things shall be whole and peaceful, because they clearly are not."

"Why couldn't God have made a world without sin, Julian? Then everything would be well. We would all love each other and work for each other's good and there would be no more pain or dying or suffering or sin."

"I've asked God that question so many times," Julian sighed. "I've found myself in tears and grief over all the pain and sorrow we see around us. 'Good Lord, how can all be well when such great hurt has come to your creatures through the evil things we do to each other?'"

"Have you received an answer?"

"No. But I have some comforting words that God put into my mind. 'I am able to make all things well. I know how to make all things well, and I shall make all things well. You will see it for yourself that I will make all things well.'"

"In other words, God is saying, 'Trust me!'"

Julian sighed and nodded agreement. "For now at least, Sister, that must be enough."

1383

I believe all
the Holy Church preaches and teaches.
I was given the faith of the Holy Church
when I was a child.
I hope, by the grace of God
to live and use that faith.
It will always be in my consciousness,
and I intend never to believe
anything that is contrary to it.

During her first months as head of Carrow Abbey, Sister Joan, or Mother Abbess as she was now known, visited Julian regularly. But then the visits became less frequent, and when she did visit, the abbess seemed tired, edgy, withdrawn.

Julian encouraged her old friend to talk about her new life, but she always quickly changed the subject. Finally, on one December afternoon, Julian confronted her directly. "Joan, you and I have been friends since our childhood. You helped me through my darkness, now you must let me help you through yours. What is happening? You look tired and thin. You are clearly unhappy. Tell me what's going on."

The abbess said nothing for a few moments, then began to get up as if to leave. "Please talk to me!" Julian pleaded.

She sat. But there were no words. Eventually some tears showed in her eyes, and then she spoke. "My church is dying."

Julian waited. With a look of hopelessness on her face that Julian had not seen before, the abbess continued. "The church I loved and trusted all my life is disintegrating. Don't you see it, Julian?"

"Yes. I see it, Joan. I see it."

"Even our Benedictine Order is disintegrating. Monks and nuns are ignoring their vows of poverty and chastity. My own nuns at Carrow Abbey are increasingly lax about our rules. As far as I know, none of them has taken a lover, but several have gone into the city alone. They don't really care if it's against our rule, or whether I approve or not. But that's not the worst of it. The whole church is in scandal. The pope, my own bishop." She wept silently. Julian reached through her window and took the abbess' hand.

"Yes, I know, Mother Abbess. I had a visit two days ago from a woman named Maggie Baxter. She's been in to see me several times. Her visits always trouble me. She's part of a group called the Lollards, followers of a man named John Wycliffe. They have many good things to teach, but Maggie is sometimes so brash, it is hard to hear the good in what she is saying."

Julian did not often talk to others about the visitors who came to her cell. She had taken no vow of confidentiality, nor did the church teach that the confidences shared with an anchorite were secret. But Julian felt she held their stories in trust. She had never spoken to Alice about it, even though Alice couldn't help but sometimes overhear the conversations. There had never been an indication from anyone that Alice had been gossiping. But now, Julian needed to talk with the abbess about Maggie.

Maggie had burst into the anchorhold and yanked back the curtain just as she had done on every visit. "That husband of mine! William's out there again getting wood with those men who talk this Lollardy stuff. It's gettin' so I don't know what to believe no more." Maggie began to sniffle. "Maybe that's why I don't have no babies. Least that's what Anna says. She says, 'Go talk to the anchorite in Norwich.'"

"Who is Anna?"

"She lives right nearby our place in Martham. Anna says she gets babies every year 'cause she hears the mass regular, every week. Ain't that somethin'? She believes everything the priest tells her. She's a little bit stupid."

"You don't believe everything the priest says?"

"Well, I got more than bull droppin's for brains. And William, he talks to his mates and some of them talk about a letter from John Wycliffe sayin' the church is doin' a wrong thing tryin' to get folks to buy them indulgences. So William, he says we ain't buyin' none of them, an' I keep wonderin' if that's why I don't get no babies."

"Maggie," said Julian gently. "You are still very young. You have many years ahead of you. I don't know why you haven't had babies, but I'm sure it has nothing to do with buying indulgences. Keep praying about it."

"William, he says I ain't supposed to come and talk to you no more. He says the bishop has got you in his pocket. 'The bishop tells her what to say,' he says, 'and if she don't say it right, he'll stick his fist in her mouth.' That's what William says."

"Do you think that's true?"

"Nah! William, he thinks like all the guys. They figure every woman has to have some man tellin' 'em what to do. William don't know it, but I don't do everything he wants neither."

"Such as?"

"Well, I brung this book for you to look at." Maggie reached down into a large leather bag and pulled out a small book with wooden binding. "William would be mad as a wet hen if he knowed I brung it to you. It's the Bible. Remember last time I told you them Lollard people were going to make a Bible in the English tongue?" She handed the book to Julian.

"Oh my!" said Julian. "Oh my, this is certainly something." She turned the book over and over in her hands, as if handling a precious and delicate treasure. "It's not the whole Bible though, Maggie,

I can tell just by looking at the size of it." Julian opened the book carefully and began to read. "Forasmuch as many have taken in hand to set forth in order a declaration of those things which are most surely believed among us..."

"Well that's English, all right," said Maggie. "But it don't make no sense."

"It's Luke's gospel. Luke's story of Jesus. He's saying that others have written the story, but he wants to tell the story his own way. Here, let me read you the story of how Jesus was born. You've heard this story many times, but now hear it in English from the Bible." Julian's finger ran down the columns of writing.

Maggie listened intently as Julian read the story of the annunciation, of the angel Gabriel coming to Mary to tell her she was to give birth to the Christ child.

"I wouldn't a done that," Maggie interjected. "Yeah, I sure want to get pregnant, but not by some angel. I'd say, 'No, thank you very much,' that's what I'd say."

"That's not what Mary said. 'Lo, I am God's handmaiden. Let it happen to me according to your word.' I've never read an English translation before." Julian smiled and closed the book slowly. "May I keep this for a while to read it?"

"Not on your flippin' life! William gets home tomorrow from his wood gatherin' trip, and tomorrow night a bunch of folks is comin' to our house and one of 'em is going to read this to us. We don't need no priest to read it to us. We don't need priests for nothin'. We can figure everythin' out for ourselves. That's what those folks are saying. Ain't that somethin'?"

"Are you saying you have no need of Holy Church?" Julian was shocked.

Suddenly Maggie seemed to shrivel. Tears welled up in her eyes. "Well, that's what I can't figure out. Them folks that come to the meetin' is sayin' we don't need the church, and we can make our own priests. Some of them was sayin' even women could be priests. But I get so scared when I hear that talkin' because supposin' they's wrong. And supposin' the bishop hears about it. That's why I brung the book, Julian. Is it okay to listen to someone readin' out of it, or are we going to cook in hell like my friend Anna says."

"I don't think you're going to cook in hell, Maggie, whether you're a Lollard or not. And I know there are many things about the church that disturb us, and that there are clergy who do evil things. But at its heart, our church is good. And there are many very good people who are priests and bishops. Don't abandon the church, Maggie. There's more good in it than there is bad. And yes, sometimes it's very hard to know what is evil and what is holy."

"I'm still scared."

"Of course. I would be too. But you have a right to your own thoughts. You said so yourself."

"That's what I keep sayin', but I don't think I really believe it. Anyways, I got to trot because there's a guy with a cart going to Martham and I can get a ride if I get out to the road right away. Can I have my book back?"

Julian handed the book carefully through the window. "I really would like to read that sometime, if it's possible. Come back when you can, Maggie. I'll pray for you and you pray for me."

"Oh, yeah. I forgot."

"What did you forget?"

"I forgot you said that even the likes of me could pray to God, and we didn't need no priest to do it for us. William tells me that's what John Wycliffe says. We don't need no priests."

"I *did* say you could pray to God yourself, Maggie. I did *not* say we had no need of priests. They are called to serve God in a particular vocation. A very difficult one. Their vocation is to lead us to God, and we need all the help we can get in doing that."

"William, he says them priests, all they want is our money. And they're all the time screwin' around."

"That's not true, Maggie. There are priests like that, but most of them are kind and generous and faithful and try very hard to serve God through their vocation. One bad apple doesn't mean the whole barrel is rotten."

"Well, my William, he says them priests is rotten!"

"Some of them are, Maggie, but not most of them. I have a brother who is a priest, and he tries very, very hard to be faithful to his calling and to live his vows."

Maggie glared at Julian. "You're like all of them, ain't you? You think the bishop's shit don't stink and you say whatever you're told to say. Well, a plague on you!"

She turned and stomped out of the anteroom before Julian could respond. But Julian made a mental note to remember Maggie in her prayers. "A girl with that kind of spark will have an interesting life," she murmured to herself.

"I've certainly heard about the Lollards," Abbess Joan said, after Julian had told her about Maggie's visits. "One of our priests told me they are all over Norfolk, and they are telling people not to give their tithe to an unworthy priest. I'm told that Wycliffe is protected by the Duke of Lancaster and by the king and others. They like what he says about kings having the final authority about who is appointed bishop or who is named as the abbot of a monastery."

"I think our bishop is worried. He must have someone watching who comes to my cell, because Father Reginald, his emissary, was on my doorstep the next day. When John Ball came by, it took him two days."

Julian had found the priest's visit upsetting, though she wasn't sure why.

"It is said that you have been instructing people to say their own prayers to God, and that they do not need the office of a priest," said the bishop's emissary. "Is that true?"

Julian had opened her curtain to him this time. He was a short man, slightly overweight, a reddish face and beads of sweat on his forehead even though the weather was cool. He reminded her of Uncle Robert.

"It is true that I have told those who visit my cell that they may pray directly to God," said Julian. "That is what Holy Church teaches, is it not?"

"It is not necessary to remind them of it, however." The priest spoke loudly and his face became more flushed. "There is enough muttering about the church as it is, without you telling people that priests are unnecessary."

"I do not say that priests are unnecessary. Priests are called to a most worthy vocation and a most difficult one too. We need priests to lead us into the loving arms of God, through the celebration of the sacraments and the preaching of the gospel."

"John Wycliffe and the Lollards are preaching that tithes should not be paid to priests who sin, and that it is not useful to contribute to the Bishop's Crusade and thereby gain forgiveness of sins."

Julian smiled sadly to herself. So many sins and heresies are tolerated, except those that keep money from church coffers. But she said nothing.

"Be careful how you instruct those gullible souls who come to you. His Grace is well aware of what you say to people." He stood to leave.

"I shall pray for you," said Julian.

"I told you last time I came and I tell you again. I do not need nor want a woman's prayers!" Father Reginald slammed the door of the anteroom on his way out.

Julian shook her head slightly to bring herself back into the present. Mother Joan was speaking again.

"We've had to cut our expenses at the abbey and the sisters are complaining. They want meat on the table every week and some want wine to drink instead of ale." She shook her head in disbelief. "But I can't squeeze more money out of our tenants. They rose up in anger just two years ago, and they will do it again if we push them unduly."

The abbess sounded desperately tired. "I might have strength to endure all this if Holy Church were not such a scandal. Imagine! Two popes excommunicating each other."

Urban VI was the pope in Rome, supported by England, and Clement VII was in Avignon, supported by France and Scotland. Each accused the other of being the enemy of the Catholic faith – the anti-Christ. The only thing they both agreed on was that armed force would be necessary to resolve the conflict.

Bishop Despenser had persuaded Pope Urban to proclaim a crusade against the pope of Avignon. And the bishop was eager to lead it. The pope had then sent missives calling on all Christians to support the crusade. Bishop Henry organized the support in England, beginning, of course, with Norwich.

Julian had been shocked and saddened as she listened to the Sunday Mass through her squint into the church. Instead of the usual pastor's homily, Father Reginald was there representing the bishop. His face flushed, he called on everyone to support the crusade against "the devil himself, the false Pope Clement"!

"All Christians are called upon to support this crusade. If you are a man, strong and youthful and trained in the manly art of war, then the bishop calls you to take the cross and follow him into this holy crusade. Holy Church has a treasury of merit, which the Holy Father will bestow on those who go to battle for the sake of Christ. If you take the cross, you will receive forgiveness of all your sins, and if you die, you will go directly to heaven. If you are not a man who can take the cross of the crusader, you can still receive such an indulgence. If you donate a sum of money to this holy cause, an amount appropriate to your station in life, you too will be granted full remission from the fires of purgatory."

It was this last offer that shocked Julian, as it had shocked the abbess. Before that time, the amount of money required to receive full remission of sins had been fixed. That was bad enough, but it was only the wealthy who bought indulgences. Now it was left up to the discretion of Despenser's commissioners, and they pressured even the poorest villeins to part with their last penny. The commissioners were given unusual powers to command the cooperation of the curate of any parish. They received a commission of sixpence on every pound they collected. Then Bishop Henry stepped up the pressure by commanding all priests to continually remind everyone, every day if possible, until they gave enough money. It became more of a shakedown than a collection.

Abuse gave rise to more abuse. In every community, bogus collectors of indulgence money appeared everywhere. In the marketplace as in the churches themselves, these commissioners accused each other of fraud. How would the average person know the difference, when they couldn't read the letters of authority both claimed to have from the bishop?

"I could hear them yelling and fighting right in the church," Julian told her friend sadly. "They called each other vile names, and I think came to blows, or at least it sounded like it. The priest was unable to finish the mass."

"They came to Carrow Abbey and even tried to get money out of the nuns, and then they demanded money from the abbey itself," said Mother Joan. "What bothered me most is that I found out some of the nuns *had* money to give – and they've taken a vow of poverty! They're not supposed to have any money at all, but here they were, digging under their beds to find sacks of coins. And they were giving it willingly. They love this fighting bishop. They think Bishop Henry is wonderful."

"They came to see me too," said Julian. "I told them I had no money – not a farthing – but they claimed that since I had been copying manuscripts, I had been paid for them. They accused me of lying. And I am getting so very tired of hearing their constant harangue in church. At every mass."

A profound silence descended over both women. Then Julian spoke again. "Do you no longer believe in Holy Church?" she asked gently. Mother Joan was silent.

"God weeps for all of us who are part of Holy Church, Mother Abbess, and loves us all the more dearly for the troubles we endure. I know. It seems…it seems as if the church is being shaken in anguish and tribulation in this world, the way we shake a cloth in the wind."

Julian could see her comments were depressing the abbess even further. "Joan! We have been friends all these years. Trust me. Believe me. When things depress and confuse us, we must trust in the mystery. God can and will turn this pain into a thing of great joy. The church, and all those in it, must feel and know this pain. It is God's way of reminding us not to put our faith in pomp and splendour, but in the love of Christ."

"I do trust you, Julian. I've prayed and I have pondered. I've prayed for strength, but I don't feel it. I feel so weak, so inadequate. I don't know which way to turn."

—

Julian worried and prayed about the state of her church. During the long solitude of each day, from early evening through to the next afternoon, the church was never far from her mind and the constant subject of her prayers.

She was delighted when the cat returned. One day, there she was, pestering Alice for food and purring on Julian's lap as she copied her manuscript. Julian wondered if it was a good omen.

Then she had a visit from her brother, Thomas. He was excited, agitated, and his announcement sounded like a challenge. "I have taken the cross, sister. I have made my pledge to Bishop Despenser, and I will go with him on crusade against the anti-Christ in Avignon. I have heard the pope's call to serve Christ in this crusade, and I am ready to give my life in this holy cause."

"No, Thomas, no!" Julian cried.

"Why, sister?" Thomas turned to face Julian, his eyes wide with anger and challenge. "Do you not follow the teaching of Holy Church?"

"Yes, Thomas, I do. Of course I do. But the crusade is not the teaching of Holy Church. It is the ambition of Bishop Despenser..."

"The bishop has his authority from the Holy Father. How dare you question the pope?"

"Thomas, please – the bishop is going to fight other Christians. God calls us to love all creation. If we withdraw our love, if we go and kill others, then we have withdrawn our love from *all* God's creation."

"Hah!" Thomas waved off her plea. "It is time for all of us to stand up and fight for Holy Church, especially against the enemies of God within the church, such as that anti-Christ – the false pope of Avignon."

"But you are a priest, Thomas. Should you not be fighting the battles of the soul, rather than with a sword? And are there not enemies of God here in England?"

"Oh indeed!" Thomas stood tall, indignation lifting his shoulders. He was still much too thin, Julian thought, and his eyes were red and angry, perhaps even a little mad. "Sister, there is a wicked man at Oxford, an evil man. Wycliffe is his name. He and his henchmen have written the gospels in English. Not Latin. Not the language of the angels, but the language of the swineherd. The gospels were entrusted to the clergy, to the doctors of the church, so that they might administer God's word as they felt appropriate, to the laity."

"Cannot we ordinary Christians understand the gospels as well?"

"No! Well, you can understand some of the simple things, which we will tell you in English, even though it is a degrading and inferior language." Scorn almost dripped from his voice. "Like those mystery plays the guilds present on Corpus Christi day. Bawdy! Lewd! I pray that our good bishop will put a stop to them. The high knowledge of God, the pure gospel of Christ, must be spoken and written in the language of God. Do you know, sister – did you know that there is another evil preacher in Oxford besides that heretic Wycliffe. Nicholas Hereford is his name. He preaches in English! In English! At Oxford, to the schoolmen, who all know the Latin!"

"I have written my visions in English, Thomas. You know that."

Thomas was silent. Julian could see the mixed emotions playing on his face. Finally he sighed. "It would have been better if you had not done that, sister. Did I not tell you to destroy that writing? But it is no matter." Then the arrogance and anger returned to his speech. "Nothing written in English, especially if it is written by a woman, is of any note. But when educated men like that false Nicholas Hereford speak or write in English, then Holy Church must silence them. With the sword or the gallows if necessary!"

Again there was silence. Julian yearned for some way to bridge the chasm that seemed to widen each time she saw her brother. She could think of nothing to say.

"Goodbye, my sister. If I do not return, do not mourn. Know that I will be in heaven with Christ and all the saints." Without the touch of a hand, or a kiss, he turned on his heel and was gone. And Julian fell to her knees and shared her tears with God.

In the end, the news was even worse than Julian feared. Bishop Henry got his troops across the Channel to Calais, then attacked several Flemish towns and defeated them easily. "God is helping us," they trumpeted. The priest at Saint Julian's told his parishioners, "The battle near Dunkirk was fought on May 25th. That is Saint Urban's Day. And when the troops stood to sing the *Te Deum* after the victory, there was a thunderstorm, which showed that God was smiling on his people. There were 12,000 of the enemy killed, but only seven English soldiers sent their souls to heaven."

Julian pulled the curtain across her squint into the church. She could listen to no more.

"What is he doing?" Julian asked Mother Joan on her next visit. "The Flemings are supporters of Pope Urban just as we are. Why is our bishop killing them?"

The abbess shrugged. She had no answer. Had she known Henry Despenser's rationale, she would have been even more despondent. Flanders was under the control of the French, who supported Pope Clement. So for Despenser to destroy the Flemings was a destruction of French resources.

The argument became more complex when Bishop Henry attacked Ypres. The siege of that city bogged down when the defences held and the English troops came down with dysentery. In the end, the English army gave up the towns it had conquered, and straggled home in shame. Bishop Henry was disgraced, impeached and imprisoned, though the other English bishops soon bought him his freedom again.

Thomas did not return. When the other "crusaders" came straggling back from Flanders, Thomas was not among them. There was no word of why.

Julian mourned for the fruitful life that might have been for this brother of hers, the one to whom she had been both mother and sister. And she mourned for the folly of kings and bishops and their futile wars, which robbed the land of food and wealth, and of brothers, sons, and husbands.

—

It would have seemed that with the botched expedition to Flanders, Bishop Despenser would have had enough adventuring. But no sooner was he out of prison than he fitted out a fleet of ships with the help of a few nobles and lay in wait to capture the Flemish wine ships from La Rochelle. "A kick against the King of France and his evil pope!" Henry crowed. The hundred Flemish ships were sent to England, and the English toasted Bishop Henry with very good wine at a very low price.

While Despenser celebrated his momentary glory, preaching friars roamed the countryside, the more eloquent ones attracting large crowds to their popular storytelling form of preaching. Conversation about their sermons, or about the activities of the Lollards, or reform of the church was everywhere in the marketplace.

Simony – the practice of selling positions in the church, such as that of priest – was the spark that gave fire to much of the talk. The ownership of a parish was often with a monastery. The church of Saint Julian belonged to Carrow Abbey. The owner, or whoever the ownership had been sold to, collected all the tithe money, and then hired a poor unlettered "bush priest" to say Mass there, usually for a small fraction of the tithes.

Julian's cell was a busy place in this tumultuous time. And it was frustrating sometimes, because those who came for counsel really wanted Julian to support their views on one issue or another. Maggie Baxter was by no means the only visitor who questioned the actions and the teachings of the church. Nor was Father Reginald the only one to demand that she hold the party line. Priests and friars, monks and mendicant preachers came into her cell in increasing numbers, adding to the steady stream of Norwich citizens who found in her an understanding soul. In a time when the church was at its lowest ebb, spiritually, ethically, morally, a wave of lay piety was sweeping across Europe.

Julian found it hard to keep her life in balance. More people came to her window than she could speak to in a day, and some of them said she should spend more time counselling and less time in solitude. She took the suggestion to heart and prayed about it at length. In the end, she knew she could not do that. Yes, she could shorten her time of silence, but in the end her counselling would suffer.

"I believe God is calling me to be an anchorite," said a middle-aged monk to Julian one day. "In my prayers, in my meditations, I hear the call over and over. How do I know it is the voice of God?"

Julian was the only anchorite in Norwich when she entered her cell. But the monk was not the first person to ask Julian about the vocation of anchorite. She neither encouraged nor discouraged them. "If God is leading you to the vocation of anchorite, speak with your spiritual director about it, and keep on praying. It is a hard life, a painful life. Only if you are absolutely certain, only if you surely know it is the call of God, should you undertake this vocation."

Alice found herself busy during these days managing the flow of traffic. She stood outside the anchorhold to be sure no one barged in on Julian when she was with another person. Often, especially if the weather was bad, she asked visitors to wait inside Saint Julian's Church. Alice enjoyed her conversations with them while they waited and some of them became her friends. Alice had never experienced friends before – friends who dropped by just for a visit.

Julian pushed herself to listen carefully to each complaint, each story, even those that oozed self-pity or raged with blame. Sometimes she had to force herself not to challenge, not to argue, but to listen with deep empathy. Most often, that was all that was needed – a kindly, listening heart. Sometimes she could offer a helpful suggestion, though many already knew what they should do and only needed to have their solutions confirmed.

A shaking, pale, middle-aged woman came running to Julian one afternoon. "They called me a witch!" she blurted out. "They said I went into the forest to have sex with the devil, but I was gathering berries for food. That's all! And they were taunting me, asking if it was true the devil's member was icy cold. What should I do? Will they burn me?" She began to cry hysterically.

Julian was often dismayed at the almost obsessive fascination with evil people showed when they came to see her. Common superstition had it that the devil could easily fool humans by taking any form at all, even the form of Christ or the Virgin Mary. Insanity, most people believed, was caused by demon possession, and many clergy found themselves in the role of exorcist.

Julian struggled to find something helpful to say to this frightened woman. "I believe you!" she said.

"You do? You don't think I'm a witch?"

"I am sure you are not a witch. Nor are you an evil person. The hard thing will be to convince your friends and family of that. I will pray for you. Not once, but long and often. What is your name?"

"Beatrice."

"I will pray for you, Beatrice. And I want you to know that God listens to prayer. So I want you to pray also. But there's something else you need to do that is going to be really hard."

"What?"

"I want you to go to your priest and..."

"No! He's one of the people who say I'm a witch. He's angry because I wouldn't go to bed with him."

"Oh, dear. That does make it difficult. Do you have a family?"

"No. I'm a widow. The priest said that because I was a widow, I must really be desperate to have a man and that I had seduced him just by the way I looked at him."

"Go to Carrow Abbey, Beatrice. I'll ask Alice, my maid, to go with you. She will take you to the abbess. Do you have any money?

"Some. My husband had been a tanner."

"I thought there was something familiar about you." Julian was glad Beatrice didn't catch her meaning. "Talk to the abbess and see if you can arrange something with her."

"You want me to become a nun?"

"I want you to be safe and happy. But I can think of worse things than becoming a nun."

Most of the problems that came into Julian's cell really had no solution. There was no divorce, no legal recourse of any kind for women who were beaten by their husbands. There was little that could be done for men, especially apprentices who were overworked and often brutally beaten by their masters. Courage, hope, and prayer was what Julian gave to them. Sometimes she would reach through the window to hold a trembling hand and listen to the sobs.

Julian was well aware that some people claimed she should always keep her curtain closed. But now she seldom closed it, except to keep the wind out. The writer of the *Ancrene Wisse* would have been scandalized, she realized. The curtain was always to be closed if the visitors were men, who might be "tempted by her feminine charms." And holding the rough hand of a man who may never have known tenderness or sympathy was not even mentioned – it was so far beyond acceptability. And yet, this sometimes seemed the most helpful part of her ministry. Just holding their trembling hands, and assuring them of God's love.

Julian often talked it over with Alice, who seemed to be a different, stronger woman since those terrifying days of the Peasants' Revolt. "Them guys who used to come to me in the whorehouse…" said Alice. "Sometimes what they wanted was just someone to hold them close, like a mother holdin' her kid. They'd get the sex thing done, real quick, and then they'd just lie there, and I would hold them tight. Sometimes I even sung to them a little. I liked it when I could lie there close to them."

"Did that happen often?"

"Nah. Two or three times, a month, maybe. But I figured if I could keep my head thinkin' about them times, maybe all the other times wouldn't seem so ugly. But then the whoremonger would bang on the door and tell me to hurry up, there was other customers waiting."

"When I think of Walter, I remember those moments of tenderness. Alice, do you think our bodies are vulgar and sinful, the way some churchmen say they are? One of the psalms says we were conceived in sin. And the priests talk about the 'filthy act' that men and women commit with each other."

"Maybe the priest only knowd about sex at a whorehouse. Yeah, that was pretty filthy. Give your money to the whoremonger. 'Lie on your back and open your legs, Alice!' Grunt! Squirt! Next! It were ugly and dirty, Mother Julian."

"Were there priests who came to your brothel, Alice?"

"Sure! Some just about every week. Three or four we seen real regular, and then some just once or twice. The whorehouse would teach 'em sex was filthy and ugly, all right."

"It's that way for some married folks too, Alice. It's not something anyone talks about, but I can see the lonely look in the eyes of both the men and women who come to me. So often they just need someone to talk to – someone to pay attention to them a little – someone who can offer a little tenderness. I don't know how they're ever going to know that God loves them, unless they can see that love in the eyes of another man or woman."

"Yeah, I seen it in their eyes sometimes. There's a couple of men I just wanted to sit and hold on my lap, 'septin they were a fair bit too big. But I could see they hadn't had no mama to love them, never, and that's what they needed so bad."

—

Almost a year after the crusade, life had settled into a comfortable rhythm again. There was not as much pressure of people coming to her window for counsel. Julian found her twenty hours a day of solitude even more enriching. And she always looked forward to the hour in the morning she devoted to copying portions of the Bible, with Joy purring contentedly on her lap. Alice listened in silence at her window as Julian said the Latin words, then translated them into English, then said each Latin word as she wrote it on the parchment. And each evening, over a light meal, they enjoyed a lively discussion about those texts.

None of the problems Julian and the abbess had agonized and prayed over were solved. If anything, the world seemed more troubled – and the church even more corrupt.

Then Thomas came back.

He slouched his way to the street in front of Julian's cell, and simply stood there. His hair had grown over his priestly tonsure. His beard was long, dirty, scraggly. His clothes reeked.

"Do you wish to speak with the anchorite?" asked Alice coming out of her room. She didn't recognize him.

"I guess," he said woodenly.

"You may go and sit in there, on the stool in her anteroom. I'll see if she's able to speak with you." Alice went inside and whispered to Julian. "There a frightful lookin' man there. He looks like he's been sleepin' in the gutter."

Julian went to her window, but she didn't open the curtain. "I am Julian, the anchorite. You wish to speak with me?"

There was no response. Julian tried again. "Do you wish to speak with me?"

"Hello, Kate!"

There was a pause. A gasp. Then the curtain flew open. "Thomas! Oh my God, Thomas!"

"I'm your baby boy, Kate. Or should I call you Holy Mother? Or are you already a saint? What does my sainted sister think of her little brother now?"

"Thomas! You're alive! Oh, thank God, Thomas!"

"Don't be so sure I'm alive, Kate. You may be looking at a ghost!" He cackled dryly at his own joke.

Julian broke into tears. "Thomas, I'm so glad to see you. I'm so glad you're alive. What happened? Why didn't you come home with the other crusaders?"

Thomas shook his head slowly, mechanically. "Scruples, dear sister. I went on the crusade to serve God, to serve the church, so I wasn't going to plunder. I wasn't going to rip the armour from dead soldiers. I wasn't going to roam the streets stealing stuff from people. I was a priest, right? I *was* a priest. A priest ordained to celebrate the mass and preach the word." He shook his head and laughed woodenly, swaying back and forth on the stool. "I didn't go to fight. I went to be a chaplain to the men, to keep them holy for their noble crusade. Well, they left me behind in Flanders because I wouldn't plunder and I had no money to buy my way back home. They left me. Everybody came back with booty. I got left behind because I was a goddamned, goody goody priest."

"That's terrible. Didn't the bishop have a way of bringing you back home..."

"The bishop? Our mighty Bishop Despenser, gallantly leading the crusaders against the good Christian heathens at Bourborg and Nieuport and Ypres? These were Christians we were killing, Kate. Christians. At Ypres, at least, they were even loyal to the right pope."

"You knew that before you left, Thomas."

"Yeah. I knew it. And it made sense then. But it stopped making sense when I started hearing the confessions of the men who went there. All they were after was booty. Money. Plunder. More than half of them, anyway. They didn't give a tinker's dam about the popes. Despenser laughed at me when I tried to tell him about it..." Thomas slumped forward and continued to sway back and forth.

"War is horrible, isn't it, Thomas?" she sighed. "It brings out the worst in people."

"You heard about our great victory at Dunkirk on Saint Urban's Day? Do you know why the battle came to a stop, dear sister? Our men couldn't climb over the huge pile of bodies. You've never seen anything so utterly hilarious as men in armour, slipping and sliding trying to climb over a mass of corpses – well some of them weren't corpses. Some were still half alive. Slipping, sliding over all the gore." Thomas was holding himself, swaying back and forth – his eyes glazed and sightless, shaking with humourless laughter. "Then we all stood and sang the *Te Deum*. It was such a wonderful victory!"

"Thomas!" Julian tried to interrupt him. "Thomas, can I have Alice get you some food, or some ale?"

"It was really comical at Ypres. Half the men got dysentery. They'd shit themselves inside their armour. The bishop made them get up and fight anyway. Some of them were so sick, they puked inside their helmets and drowned. It was so funny, Kate!" Thomas gave another dry, chilling laugh.

"How did you get home, Thomas?" Julian was trying to change the subject.

"Well, sister dear, when you're starving, you learn to steal. When you're desperate, you learn to lie. Your baby brother turned into an animal, Kate. I slept in the bush, eating whatever I could steal. It took me almost a year to get to the coast, and then I killed a man…"

"Oh, Thomas!"

"Oh Thomas!" he mocked. "Don't 'Oh Thomas' me. I did what I had to do to get a boat, and I damn near died getting across the Channel. Then I had to walk all the way from Yarmouth. Now I'm here, and I wonder why?"

"Why, Thomas? Because I love you. I do, Thomas. I really do."

"Bull shit! I'm not your brother. Your brother died in Flanders."

"My brother is sitting right here, speaking to me. We'll get you some food, and some clean clothes…"

"Shut up, Kate!"

"Then why did you come home?"

"Home? I have no idea. None."

"But you're a priest, Thomas…"

"Goodbye, Kate. That's what I came to say. Goodbye, big sister…"

"No, Thomas. Please! Please don't leave…"

But it was too late. He was gone.

The second grieving was worse than the first. Slowly, Julian felt herself slip into her melancholia, the darkness she thought she had overcome. Sliding down into her personal hell, she had only one word on her lips, over and over. "Why?"

At times Alice and the abbess wondered if she would live, and Julian hoped that she would die. "I can't leave her, abbess," said Alice. "Can you have food sent over from the abbey, and a lot of your St. John's Wort?"

It took every trick Alice had learned. All her skill. Her power. Shouting sometimes. Encouraging. And praying. Praying and still being surprised sometimes when she rose from her knees knowing her prayers were heard.

Weeks went by. Then months. Alice spoke to the people who came by the window, gave them what help she could, assured them that Mother Julian would recover, but no, she could not speak with them. But still the word went around Norwich that their beloved anchorite was dying. Alice prayed, forced Julian to drink the brewed herbs, to eat a little. Alice talked to her, joked with her, yelled at her sometimes.

Until one day Alice heard the words that sounded sweeter than any she had ever heard before.

"I'm hungry, Alice."

—

"Bishop Henry was ridin' past the market today," Alice announced as she returned with a basketful of food. "As usual, he was dressed to the teeth in his church clothes."

"You don't like him much, do you, Alice? I only saw him once, when he installed me in this anchorhold. But you've seen him four or five times in various processions and parades through Norwich. What do you think of him?"

"I don't like him real well. He's kinda pushy. Once when he was riding through town with all his flunkies, he looked like a kid I once saw wearing his dad's hat and yelling, 'Hey, mom! Look at me!' Lately the bishop's been lookin' kinda old. I wonder if he's got anyone to love him – to care for him. Seems to me all he's got are the priests he trots around with. Not much of a family, I don't think."

"You think a lot about family, don't you?"

Alice sighed and nodded.

"Neither you nor I were given much love by our mothers or fathers when we were children, Alice. You were left on a church doorstep. My father died in the great pestilence, and my mother was so angry at God, she had no room in her heart to love me."

"Yeah. I had a big lump of hate in my craw about my mama and papa too. I wanted a family real bad and I figured it was God's fault that I got dropped on the church steps and wound up in the whorehouse. Y'know what made a difference? The day, when all the villeins were fighting all over Norwich. You yelled at me, remember? And you told me to pray as if God heard me and loved me. I was so scared you were going to kick me out into all the fightin' and I'd have to go back to the whorehouse. So I done what you said, and I told God that whoever my papa and mama was, that I weren't mad at 'em no more, and after a few days of that kind of prayin', it got true. God started feelin' to me like the mama I never had."

Alice looked at Julian through the window, and saw her own tears reflected in Julian's face.

"Oh, Alice, I am so glad. I didn't know that truth either until I'd been here in the anchorhold for a while. I was so frightened at first of being alone here. No mother or sister or husband to hold me when I felt broken. But then it felt as if God became my natural mother, and God became my natural father, and it turns out to be even better than any love my mother or father could have given me."

"You ever think of gettin' married again?"

"Yes. I've sometimes wondered what life with John Ball might have been like; if he had not been a priest and I had not been an anchorite. Do you think of marriage, Alice?"

"Oh, yeah! You know somethin' funny? After praying for the whoremonger during the fighting, I realized I kinda liked the little bugger. He's the only guy I ever thought anythin' about."

"What if there was another man?"

"Nah! I got nothin' to give a guy for marryin' me." Alice shook her head and laughed bitterly. "And who would marry an old whore with her innards all twisted from that crap they made me drink when they thought I was havin' a baby. I ain't no use to nobody."

"That's not true, Alice. You came here to be my maid, but you have stayed to be my sister. I would have run screaming from this anchorhold long ago, if you hadn't been here."

"Even if you've got God as your father and mother?"

"God is not just our mother and father. God is also a beloved wife, a beloved husband, a sister, and a brother."

"So?"

"You and I and everyone else are made of the same stuff that God is made of, and sometimes it is hard to see God except in the eyes of another human being. Sometimes it is through another human being that we can hear God say, 'I love you, and you love me. This love will never be broken.' And often, especially since those days when all the fighting was going on, you have shown me the face of God."

Alice waved her hand dismissively and made a face.

"No, don't react like that, Alice! It is true! You are not the only one. I have seen God in the faces of many people who came to my cell, just as I have seen evil in some of their faces. I saw God in the face of my mother the night she lay here dying. I've seen God in the face of Mother Cecily and Mother Joan."

"Mother Joan ain't lookin' too chipper, is she?"

"Life has been very hard for her this last while. Very hard." Julian paused and shook her head sadly. Then she brightened. "Alice! I have an idea. If you have enough money, go to the market and buy a small jug of good wine. And if you can find some good cheese in the market, get that too. Put them in your bag, then go to visit Mother Joan. Tell the sister at the door that you have a private message from Mother Julian. Then, when you're alone together, tell her you are returning the jug of wine and the cheese Mother Cecily sent us when we first moved into the anchorhold. And if she wants to talk, just sit and listen."

"You ain't never asked me to do nothin' like this before. You're askin' me to go and help the abbess? Me?"

"Yes, Alice. You."

1394

And then our gentle Lord
showed me a mysterious parable
about a lord who has a servant.
The lord sits in rest and in peace.
The servant stands before the lord reverently,
ready to obey.
As soon as the lord makes a request,
the servant races off, pell-mell,
falls into a muddy ditch
and is badly hurt.
I looked to see if the lord would blame the servant for this,
but there was no blame to be seen.

Alice stood at the window between her room and Julian's anchorhold. She was soaking wet. One eye was swollen shut. Her right hand was bruised and bloodied.

"Dear Alice! Whatever happened to you?"

"I shouldn't a taken the shortcut through the alley. I heard lotsa times that people get knocked off goin' through there. But I ain't never had nothin' so important to do before, and I figured if I saved a bit of time I could sooner get to go and see the Mother Abbess right in her own place. But these two guys jumped me."

"That's how you got the swollen eye and the bruise on your hand?"

"Yeah! I don't know if they wanted my money or if they was tryin' to rape me. But I gave one of 'em a haymaker in the snout. That's how I got my hand all mashed up. I think I broke it. He run off howlin'. Then the other one come at me and punched me in the eye, but I gave him a good sharp kick in the family jewels." Alice grinned. "Not bad for an old crone, eh?"

"Do you know who they were?"

"Sure. I don't know their names, but I seen them hangin' around the marketplace. They're a couple a small-time thieves. They won't come after me no more."

"Don't be too sure of that, Alice. Men don't like to be bested in a fight, especially by a woman – especially by an older woman – and they may try for revenge. Please be careful."

"Yeah. Anyhow, I got the wine and went as fast as I could to Carrow Abbey, and the nun at the door of Mother Joan's house kinda looked me up and down. She didn't like the look of me, bloodied up and dress torn, and I can't say's I blame her. So she wanted to know what my name was and who sent me and how come I looked so beat up. Then she went inside, I guess to ask Mother Abbess if it was okay.

"It's a swell house the abbess lives in. Painted walls and three chairs to sit on. She even has a fireplace in the wall, and it has a chimney to take the smoke up. There weren't no smoke at all in her room. And they bring her lotsa firewood so's she can keep warm the whole winter." Alice's face became more serious. "She ain't well, Julian. Mother Abbess is lookin' thin and sick. But she's a real nice person. She talked to me as if I was just as good as her."

"Which you are, Alice. I keep telling you that." There was a note of mild exasperation in Julian's voice. Then a flash of delight. She noticed that Alice had called her Julian. She decided not to say anything about it, in case it was a mere slip of the tongue. But Julian hoped she would never hear Alice call her "ma'am" again.

"I know, Julian," Alice continued, "but sitting there with just one eye open and dirty and smelling of sweat, it's kinda hard to believe that. But we talked for a long time, about all kinds a stuff. And she liked the wine. She said it was exactly the medicine she needed. She even gave me some of it, but I didn't like it much."

"I see she sent my book."

"Yeah, but jeez, I'm sorry. It was rainin' like stink all the way home and coldern' a witch's tit. I was runnin' because I wanted to get back here as fast as I could. And I slipped on the street and dropped your book in a puddle. I think I wrecked it."

"Don't worry, Alice. We'll find some rags to clean it off. Did Mother Joan say why she sent my book? I had given it to the abbey."

"No. I even asked her, but she just said it was time the book went home."

Julian picked up her book and thumbed through it. It brought a rush of memories, and a sense of gratitude to Joan, her lifelong friend who had seen her through so much of her fifty-two years. "Alice, I think Mother Joan needs more visits from you. The only people she sees are her own nuns, and they all say the same predictable things. Go see her as often as you can. Just sit with her and talk."

Carefully, Julian wiped the mud and dried the pages of her precious book. She'd thought little about the book over the years. The former abbess had kept it in her own room where she sometimes showed it to visitors. Occasionally, someone would mention it to Julian. Few people could read, except for priests and monks, and they had no interest in a book written in the coarse Norfolk English dialect and by a woman.

She was glad of the continuing rain during the next few days. It kept at home those who didn't absolutely need to go out, and only a few people came by her window. So Julian read. Her own words they were, but sometimes it almost felt as if they were written by another person. She resisted the temptation to change the words, especially when she repaired those words that had been smudged by water.

Some of the words brought her up short. "For your own good, disregard the wretched worm, the sinful creature to which it was shown. Because I am a woman, must I therefore believe that I should not tell you of the goodness of God?" Who was that poor trembling child who penned those words twenty years ago? She certainly didn't see herself as a "wretched worm" any longer. But most of the other words rang true, still, and Julian was more convinced than ever that her revelations were a gift from God. And her book was good, as far as it went. But there was so much more to be said, so much more that she had learned from prayer and meditation, and from the people who came to her window.

Julian remembered the parable she had left out of her first book, the parable of the lord and the servant. She stood up and looked through the window to the room where Alice was awkwardly preparing a meal with her left hand, her right hand raw and blue looking and held carefully out of the way, her left eye still swollen shut. Julian watched her friend and companion and realized how much she loved this big-boned woman with her coarse talk, her sometimes childish ways, and the deep and desperate hurt she carried from her terrifying childhood. Alice had not acted out the parable for her, but she had unknowingly shone a light on it. Suddenly, the story of the lord and the servant, a revelation she had puzzled over and prayed about for twenty years, was clear to her. Or almost. She must write it down.

Julian paced around her cell, the thoughts crowding each other in her mind. She still had a few scraps of parchment and leftover writing supplies from the various manuscripts she had copied for the cathedral priory, and on these she wrote the essence of each thought, each insight, each revelation, lest she forget the things God seemed to be revealing to her – insights God had given her over the years. None of these thoughts were her own; Julian was convinced of that. They were gifts given from God and must be shared.

Alice passed the simple evening meal through the window to Julian. Boiled cabbage, dark bread, and a mug of ale. Julian crossed herself. "Thank you, Alice. Tomorrow, if it isn't raining, please go back to Carrow Abbey to see Mother Abbess, and thank her for sending me my book. Then tell her also that I believe God wants me to write more words, many more words, so I will need more quills, ink, and parchment."

The rain was steady and strong and drenching the next morning. A strong wind from off the North Sea blew it in sheets against the anchorhold. As soon as it was light enough to see, Julian heard Alice leaving. "I should have waited till I saw what the weather was like before I asked her to go to Carrow," Julian thought to herself in the middle of her morning prayers. "Now there's no stopping her."

Alice was back three hours later, drenched and cold. Late that afternoon over their meal together, Alice explained. "Mother Joan says she doesn't have much writing stuff at Carrow, but she would send a messenger to get it from the cathedral priory."

"How was she?"

"She was smiling. There was better colour in her face. But she is so frightful skinny!"

"She is very ill, I think, Alice. Do go back to her every week. More often if she seems to want it. Joan needs you."

—

A messenger arrived in a horse-drawn cart the next afternoon, and Alice helped him unload. It seemed like a huge pile of parchment – nice white sheepskin it was too. And ink and quills. "Enough here to write all the words in the world," remarked the messenger.

"We'll have to be careful this parchment doesn't get wet and start rotting," Julian said to Alice. "You'll need to check it and perhaps air it out every week or so."

Julian could hardly wait. The next morning she gathered the scrap bits of parchment on which she had written her notes. She'd even written on a piece of timber in her cell when she ran out of scraps of parchment – anything to help her remember her thoughts which seemed to come in such profusion sometimes.

She could hardly control the trembling in her hand. Now, after so many years, she felt she understood the parable of the lord and the servant, which she had left out of her earlier book of showings. Inside this parable, she hoped, were the answers to the questions that had troubled her in writing the first book.

Julian sat in the stillness, pen in hand, focusing on the memory of a vision, a vision she had revisited so many times since it first came to her. Then she wrote.

"The lord sits solemnly in rest and peace, while the servant stands reverently nearby, ready to do his will.

"The lord looks upon his servant with love and gentleness, and then quietly he asks him to go on an errand. The servant not only goes, but he starts out running because of the love he has, and his eagerness to do whatever the lord asks. And almost right away he trips and falls into a deep swampy pit, and gets himself badly injured in the process. He lies there, groaning and hurting, and hard as he tries, he just can't stand up and get himself out of that hole.

"The only thing the servant did wrong, when he was down in the ditch, was that he didn't turn his face and see his lord who was close by and ready to help him.

"Then I looked at him closely to see if I could see anything he had really done wrong, or whether the lord would blame him for what he had done. But I didn't see anything like that. It was the servant's good will, his enthusiasm that had caused the fall. And that's why the lord kept looking at him with great love and tenderness."

Julian smiled, thinking of poor Alice standing in the doorway, with her sore hand and her eye swollen shut. She remembered the intense love she had for this woman. As far as everyone else was concerned, Alice was her servant and Alice saw herself that way. But in Julian's heart, Alice was a sister.

The parable of the lord and the servant would become the key chapter in her new book, she realized. Through this parable, Julian could understand how God became a human in the person of Jesus. And if she could understand that, perhaps she would also understand the questions that had troubled her for as long as she could remember. Why do such evil things happen? How could the Black Death have happened? How can all be well when there are two popes, each claiming to be the Vicar of Christ, each one hurling insults at the other?

Julian had struggled with these kinds of questions for twenty years. If God is all goodness, then it is impossible for God to be angry, because if God were angry, even for a second, the whole of creation would be destroyed. God is love. She had heard God's promise very clearly: "All shall be well!" And in her visions, she had not seen sin. It wasn't just that it had been left out, she was convinced that sin had no substance. No reality of its own.

But that was nonsense. The memory of her brother Thomas flashed through her mind. He was enthusiastic but naïve, just like the servant in her story. He'd gone to Flanders full of faith and good will. He came back a hollow shell. "And where are you now, Thomas?" she whispered.

Anyone can see that things are not well, that terrible things happen, that people constantly sin. All of them. Julian was keenly aware of her own sin. Not the spectacular sins of the market or the palace or the brothel, but the everyday sins of envy, anger, pride, fear, boredom. Julian faced those every day, and some days they almost consumed her. Over the years she had been in the anchorhold, she knew there were many times when she came within a whispered prayer of screaming her way out of her prison. And she would have done it too, if it hadn't been for the firm and kindly care of Alice. God has sent Alice, of that she was sure.

Julian closed her eyes to recall once again the parable of the lord and the servant, but instead she remembered a long ago conversation with Alice.

"The farmer made me take them ticks off'n the cows' backs," Alice had explained. "Them cows didn't like it, cause them ticks had dug theyselves in and to get 'em out I hadda cut right into the cow's skin. Funny, the cows let me do it to them. I'd talk to them quiet like, and their eyes would get real big, but they wouldn't kick or butt. They'd raise holy hell when the farmer tried to do it. One of them cows nearly killed him once. Maybe 'cause I slept in the barn with 'em. Maybe they thought I was just a weird lookin' cow. And I felt sorry for 'em. I didn't like hurtin' 'em. I think them cows kinda knowed that. Maybe they knowed we had to get them ticks out or them cows would die. They'd get more and more ticks on their hides, and they'd suck all the blood out of 'em."

"So the ticks would kill the cow eventually," Julian said. "But then the ticks would die themselves if the cow died?"

"Yeah, sure. Funny, ain't it? Them ticks need the cows to feed on, but then they kill the cow by doin' that. Sort of like the whoremonger. He needed the women in his whorehouse to lay down for ten, twenty guys in a night, and it was killin' us. And if his whores all died, the whoremaster would die too."

Julian wondered why she thought about that conversation just then. Perhaps God had sent her that memory to help her understand the nature of sin. Maybe sin has no substance, no reality of its own, but is a parasite that feeds on goodness. "Sin is necessary," she said to herself, "because without sin, there would be nothing for people to choose except goodness, and that would be no freedom – no goodness at all. Sin feeds on the goodness God created in us and in the world. But if we let sin have its way – if we don't cut it out – it will kill us. That cutting hurts, and like Alice's cows, we kick and fight when it happens. Sin can suck the life out of us. But it has no life of its own. When our goodness has been sucked out of us by sin, then the sin dies as we die."

This insight on the nature of sin, Julian realized, had to do with the parable of the lord and the servant, and that it all connected to the story of Adam and Eve, and to the coming of Jesus. Julian picked up the pen and wrote some more, then put it down again. "How can I say all this so that my ordinary Christians can understand it?"

She stopped to pray and to meditate. Then she wrote some more. "I looked all around, everywhere I could think of, but I could not see any help for the servant. Then this kind lord said, 'See my beloved servant, all the pain and hurt he has had to experience because he tries so hard to do all I ask him. He does it for love. He does it for me. So it seems right that I should give him some reward for all his fear, his injuries, his pain. And does it not seem right that the reward should somehow make up for the injury and hurt that he's experienced? If I didn't do that, I'd be most ungracious.'

"But how can I make sense of all this?" Julian found herself wondering. "How do I understand it myself?" As had been her practice when she first wrote her first book, she stopped repeatedly to ask God for guidance. And again she received an inward instruction.

"Pay close attention to all the details," God seemed to say to her. "Every colour, shade, gesture, or action has meaning, even if at first they seem to you mysterious and vague."

Julian realized she needed to meditate on the parable as if it were an allegory. Everything in the story had significance – the colours, the postures, the way the servant stood in relationship to the lord, the clothes they wore. Everything stood for something else. What's more, every detail stood for some significant connection with the biblical story. And hidden within the story was a deeper and more profound meaning.

Julian soon realized that the servant in her story initially stood for Adam, who sinned mightily and fell into hell. But at the end of her parable, the servant had become the Christ, who fell into Mary's womb.

By looking at the details of the story, Julian found herself understanding a bit more. After he was rescued from the swampy pit, the servant wanted to do something wonderful for the lord whom he loved so much. He planted a garden and grew some delicious food. "The servant knew he was to keep on doing his best in his work," Julian wrote. "He was to irrigate his garden, and make good, sweet fruit grow. And he was to bring this to his lord, prepared just the way the lord liked it."

Julian put down her pen. She didn't like this story. It seemed very selfish to her, that the lord should want the servant to work so hard, especially since the danger of falling into that ditch again was always there. Then her meditation took her back to memories of her own children, and how they had sometimes wanted to make something special for her or for Walter.

Julian remembered a little straw doll that little Maud had made with great love. She had helped the child find the straw. Walter provided some thin strips of leather, and little Maud held the straw while Walter tied the knots. It was a strange looking doll when all was said and done, but little Maud was so pleased to give the doll to Katherine, and she in her turn was delighted as a mother to receive this gift of love.

The lord in Julian's story is delighted that the servant wants to express his love, and doesn't brush aside his efforts. But why then did the lord allow the servant to fall into a ditch? For the same reason Katherine allowed Maud to cut the straw herself with a sharp knife. Katherine watched and worried that the child might hurt herself.

"Ah! Now I've got it!" Julian whispered. The gift is meaningless if there is no danger, no struggle, no hardship involved.

But humans have a hard time grasping this, so God becomes human. God took on human form in Christ. And in doing this, God showed us a nurturing, mothering side. God comes and lives with us. "Like Alice living in the barn with the cows," Julian smiled to herself.

And what about the end of the parable? The servant is beautifully clothed, sitting with God who is full of glory and joy. And in the vision Christ says to Julian, "If you are satisfied, I am satisfied. It is a joy, a bliss, an endless delight to me that ever I suffered my Passion for you; and if I could suffer more, I would suffer more."

Julian smiled. She suddenly realized that our human journey through pain and death is not a punishment for sin. It is the way things have to be for humans, who can choose between good and evil. She began to hum the old song:

Blessed is the time
That apple taken was.
And that is why we sing
'Deo Gracias!'

Having completed the story of the lord and the servant – the longest chapter she had ever written – Julian realized that her first book really was a prelude to this parable. She would copy most of that first book again, she decided, and make it the beginning of her new book. Then she would tell the parable and explain what it meant.

But as Julian began to copy her first book, she found herself unhappy with parts of it. Some of the revelations were not well expressed when she wrote the first book. She frowned as she read the snivelling passage about being a woman and not worthy to write a book. "God called me to write this book, and it doesn't matter if some of the churchmen don't like it," she muttered.

It took longer to copy the first book into the second than Julian expected. She could write quickly now, but it was a cold winter, and though Alice built a small fire in the pit in the centre of the anchorhold on the coldest days, Julian's aging fingers were growing arthritic. She missed the warmth of Joy, her cat. Joy would sleep and purr on her lap as she wrote, and Julian would warm her hands on its fur. But Joy had died of old age some years earlier.

To Julian's frustration, the quill often slipped from her fingers or she dropped big ugly blobs of ink onto the parchment. "Perhaps my writing and copying days are done," she thought.

On these winter days that turned so quickly into night, Julian tried sometimes, if there was no visitor at her window, to work in the late afternoon by the feeble, smoky light of an acrid tallow candle.

"I guess God doesn't want me to write then," she said to Alice. "The light is best in the late morning, so that's when I'll write."

Alice agreed. "Besides, a one pound tallow candle costs a day's wages."

In the end, Julian realized she was glad of the time during the long nights of winter. She wrote in the daylight, then reflected in the darkness – reflected on her own words and prayed for insight. Most often, she used the time of darkness to replay in her mind the parable of the lord and the servant. Gradually, the story revealed its inner meaning to her.

"God almighty is our natural father," she wrote, "and God all-wisdom is our natural mother, who together with the love and goodness of the Holy Ghost are all one God, one Lord. In the knitting and the uniting God is our own true spouse. We are God's beloved wife. 'I love you and you love me, and our love shall never be divided,' God says to us.

"Thus in our father, God almighty, we have our being. In our merciful mother, through whom our parts are united and made perfect, we have our reforming and our restoration. Our essence is our father, God almighty. Our essence is our mother, God all-wisdom. Our essence is our lord the Holy Ghost, God all-goodness."

It was not a totally new thought. Julian had encountered such ideas in some of the books she had read or copied, of God having the attributes of a mother. That thought had been in her mind for many years, though she'd never heard of a mothering God in the homilies she listened to through the squint into Saint Julian's Church.

It was a hard thing to explain. "No," she said over and over when she spoke of a mothering God and "our mother Jesus" to people who came to her window. "I have not said that God is a woman. Nor have I said that God is a man. You see, God isn't a human being like you and me. It really doesn't make sense to talk about God as either male or female. Motherliness is part of the nature of God. Jesus cared for us the way a good mother cares for her children."

But now she took the idea even further. "The mother's service is nearest, readiest, and surest," she wrote, "for it is the truest, and cannot really be done except by God alone. We imagine that our mothers bear us only to pain and to death, but our own mother Jesus, who is all love, bears us to joy and endless life.

"The mother may give her child her milk to suck, but our beloved mother Jesus feeds us with himself. He does this so gently and lovingly with the blessed sacrament, which is the priceless food of life itself. Mercifully and graciously he sustains us with all the sweet sacraments.

"The kind loving mother knows and understands the needs of her child. She protects it most tenderly, in keeping with her nature as a mother. As the child grows, she changes the way she relates to the child, but she doesn't change her love.

"The mother may let the child fall sometimes. The child might be worried about what is going to happen. But because she is a mother, she will never let any kind of danger harm her child. Although an earthly mother may have to endure the death of her child..."

Julian stopped. The rush of memory overwhelmed her, and again she shed the tears still left in the well of sadness that held the memory of her two babies. And finally, these many years later, she breathed a thanks to God for the short time she had them, and commended them to God's love and safekeeping. "And tell them please, that it won't be long before their earthly mother comes to join them."

Then she finished the sentence. "...our heavenly mother Jesus will not allow those of us who are his children to perish – for he alone is almighty, all wisdom and all love."

It took Julian much more time to write her second book, not only because it was longer, but because she had to think each thought through carefully. Sometimes, when she read over the parts that she had written, she needed to do it all over again – sometimes whole chapters.

Finally, the last chapter, number eighty-six.

"This book was begun by God's gift and grace. But it is still not complete." Julian knew that her writing raised as many questions as it answered. Most importantly, she knew that the holy mystery she had tried to describe was not a puzzle to be solved, but a well to which we may go, over and over, for renewal and refreshment. She also knew that the faith she had described had to be lived in her life and the life of others before it would be complete.

Her terrible "Why?" questions were still there, but they had moved to a place of much less importance in her mind. They still woke her in the middle of the night sometimes, or intruded on her meditations. But that was less often, and when it happened she would say to herself, "Sin is inevitable. It is part of God's world. Pain and suffering happen. It is part of God's world. Injustice happens. It is part of God's world. But in God's eternal wisdom, in God's good time, I know that all shall be well. And all shall be well. And all manner of thing shall be well."

So Julian picked up her pen, and in a burst of inspiration, wrote the final words.

Would you know our Lord's meaning in all this?
Learn it well.
Love was the meaning.
Who showed it you? Love.
What did God show you? Love.
Why did God show it to you? For love.
Hold fast to this and you shall learn and know more about love,
but you shall never learn anything except love from God.
So I was taught that love was our Lord's meaning.
And I saw full surely that before ever God made us,
God loved us.
This love was never quenched, nor ever shall be.
And in this love God has created everything that is.
And in this love God has made all things for our benefit.
And in this love is our life everlasting.
And all this shall we see in God without end –
which Jesus grant us.
Amen.

Julian put her pen slowly onto her writing desk. She looked at the page she had just written and tears filled her eyes. This was why God had called her into the anchorhold. This was her *opus Dei*, her work of God. "Perhaps," she wondered, "it is now my time to die."

She heard Alice come in through the outside door, and saw her tear-stained face appear in the window. "Oh, Julian. I just come from seein' Mother Joan. She's dyin'! The sisters are all on their knees prayin' and they said to me to come tell you to pray too."

Julian went to her stool and sat. She needed to sit for a moment with the news that her old friend was dying. So many years – so much life they had shared – the prayers, the laughter as young girls – the tears and struggles and the joys of all the years. Julian closed her eyes and whispered a prayer of thanks for the gift of her friend Joan.

"Alice," she said. "Both of us must pray for Mother Joan. Let's not ask God to make her well. Let's just pray that God's love will be with her and fill her with strength in whatever is going to happen. Let's pray the way we prayed during the peasants revolt and just hold our friend in our hearts and say, 'Thy will be done.' And let's not forget to say 'Thank you' to God for her life."

Julian moved toward her kneeler, then turned and came back to the squint. "Alice," she said urgently. "Please, take this book. The pages aren't bound together yet, but the writing is finished. Wrap it up and take it to Mother Joan, and tell her the book is a gift to her and to the sisters at Carrow Abbey. You can pray while you are walking."

Suddenly Julian realized how old Alice looked. When had the tall, muscled, awkward young girl grown into a strangely graceful old woman? How had time raced by so quickly? And if Alice was getting old and Mother Joan was dying, it must mean that she was old herself. Julian had never really thought much about her own age before.

Mother Joan was only able to read a little of Julian's new book. Then she had one of the attending nuns read portions of it to her – as much as her failing energy would allow. She had the last chapter read several times.

"Send a message to my old friend, Julian the anchorite," she whispered. "Tell her this. 'All shall be well, and all shall be well. And all manner of thing shall be well.'"

The abbess had the pages of the book, with those words at the top, placed on the small table beside her bed. It was there when she died a few days later with Alice at her side, holding her hand.

1413

If there is someone who loves God,
who has never fallen down,
it wasn't shown to me.
For in God's eyes we don't fall
but in our own eyes we can't even stand up.
Both of these are true.
But God's way of seeing is the highest truth,
and God wants us to believe more
in that high understanding.

Julian had completed her writing. She did no more copying of texts. Her hands simply could not hold a quill any longer and her seventy-one-year-old eyes could no longer see the words, even when the summer sunlight streamed through the oiled linen windows. But the rhythm of her prayers and meditation continued, and in the afternoons, people kept coming to her window, looking for counsel – hungering for hope.

Some asked for the secret of her long life. At seventy-one, she had lived much longer than most people, especially most women. "I have no secret," she would laugh. "And I have no idea why I have lived so long." She flatly rejected the idea that she was God's favourite. "God loves every one of us. One just as much as the other."

Julian could no longer remember many of the people who came to her window, but she knew she would never forget Margery Kempe and Maggie Baxter.

They were two very different people – Margery and Maggie. Both of them were confused and anxious – one struggling to be the perfect churchwoman, the other moving into a strange and dangerous way of thinking. Between the two of them, they showed the temper of the times, troubled as they were.

Margery Kempe, thin and anxious, bustled into Julian's anteroom one rainy afternoon. The first thing Julian noticed was the way her eyes darted around, never resting anywhere for long. She wore a white gown, which was unusual. Well, no longer white – more a dappled grey, with the edges worn and ragged. Julian watched her intently, and waited for her to speak.

"I am Margery Kempe and I have heard say that – that you are a wise and kindly counsellor. Is that so?"

"That is not for me to judge. What brings you here, Margery?"

"Our Lord Jesus Christ has – has told me to bear no more children." She spoke with a high tremolo, constantly looking around her, seldom engaging Julian's eyes. "And to come here to Norwich and seek – seek the – the consolation of Dame Julian." Margery never seemed to end a sentence, and snatched quick little breaths in the middle of phrases – sometimes in the middle of words. "And I have come here to tell you of the sweet grace our Lord has put into my soul, of contrition, devotion, compassion with high – high meditation and high contemplation."

"With all those gifts," said Julian, slightly taken aback by the staccato torrent of Margery's declaration, "what is it you need from me?"

"I need you to tell me if there is any – any deception in my soul, for I have heard say that you are expert in such things and can give good – good advice."

"Then it would be useful if you told me some of your story," Julian said, trying to calm Margery with her voice. "Where have you come from and where are you going?"

"I come from Bishop's Lynn where my father has been mayor – mayor five times and I am married to John, a burgess of lower rank and meager wealth and I was married to him when I was twenty – twenty years of age, and as nature would have it, I was with child very – very quickly and I was much sick with the child, and what with all the labor pains, I des – despaired of my life. I thought I would die, so I sent for the priest and tried to con – confess, but the devil wouldn't let me and the devil kept telling me that I didn't need to confess and I saw devils – devils with their mouths lit up with flames as if they would swallow me and I shouted and screamed terrible words – words at my husband and all the house – household, and I would have killed myself many times if they had not kept me tied – tied up night and day and I even bit myself so hard, you can still see – see the scar." She held her hand up for Julian to see through the window.

"How long did this madness hold you?"

"Half a year, eight weeks and odd – odd days." Margery's shoulders drooped in sadness. "But then the Lord Jesus appeared to me in the likeness – likeness of a man, the most beautiful man I have ever seen." Margery stopped. Her eyes took on a faraway, romantic look. "He came and sat on the edge of my bed and spoke to me. 'Daughter, why have you forsaken me? I didn't forsake you.' And then I was as calm and clear-headed as ever – ever before."

"Did the madness return?"

"No – no, not that madness – instead – instead I went about the town showing everyone my fine, well-fashioned clothes and I wore – I wore gold pipes on my head, and my hoods – hoods with the tippets that were fashionably slashed and my cloaks were also mod – modishly slashed and underlain with many colours between the slashes and everyone looked at me and all the women were jealous."

Julian noticed a change in Margery's manner. She tossed her head and minced her shoulders as she described the latest fashion of her time. The gold pipes were also called the "crispine," a headdress made of gold wire and mesh. It was often shaped into elaborate "horns."

"You enjoyed being the envy of all the people of Lynn?"

"Yes, and I wanted so much to be respected by people." Her shoulders drooped again. "But I had not learned the lesson of my mad – madness and I demanded more money from my husband to buy clothes, and I even took up brewing ale to earn money for my folly but that business failed – failed miserably, so I bought a mill and hoped to earn money grinding corn, but that failed too and it was the Lord punishing me for my pride – pride and covetousness."

"So then you gave away all your fine clothes?"

"Yes. No. Not right away. But one night – in the middle of the night, I heard a sound, so mel – mel – melodious and sweet, so delectable, I thought I had been in paradise and I jumped out of bed and said, 'I'm sorry I sinned, because it is really wonderfully merry in heaven.'"

"You thought the sound was from heaven?"

"Oh yes, and now, anytime I hear a beautiful melody or see people being – being happy, I break out into great sobs and crying and sighing." The tremolo in her voice seemed to be increasing.

"How do you know that was a heavenly sound, Margery?"

"What? Are you just like the rest of the people that say to me, 'How do you know what heaven is like? You haven't been there!' And then they laugh – laugh at me, just as you are laughing at me now."

"I'm not laughing at you, Margery." Again Julian tried to calm Margery with the calmness of her own voice. "But if you want good counsel from me, you must be willing to answer the hard questions. How does your husband respond to all this?"

"John? Oh, he moans and – and groans. I told him I didn't want to lie with him anymore and that all my love and affec – affection was given to Jesus and I told him I'd rather drink the ooze out of the gutter than lie with him."

"I'm sure he was delighted to hear that!" Julian immediately regretted her sarcasm and was relieved that Margery didn't pick it up.

"John got up on his high horse and told me that I owed him sex and it's a debt of marriage according to the law, he says, and so I –

I obey him and I weep and cry all the time he is doing it to me but I kept – kept at him, trying to tell him that we both need to escape the sin of lust, and so three or four years after – after that, he agreed to live chastely."

"Why is that so important to you?"

"Do I need to explain that to you? You, an anchorite, a vir – virgin, you don't need to worry about such things. I have to fight the sin of lust every day."

"Is it a sin to lie with your husband, Margery?"

"It is dirty and filthy and no one can be holy – holy unless they are pure and you can't be pure if you lust for someone's body."

"You would like to be a virgin, wouldn't you? You are wearing a white dress, which is usually the symbol of virginity. Do you hope that with your many prayers God will make you a virgin somehow, like Mary, the mother of Jesus?"

Margery looked hard at Julian, then burst into tears. Great heaving sobs, loud, screaming wails, dripping wet sniffles wiped on the sleeve of her once white dress. Alice poked her head in through the window across the room, a concerned look on her face. Julian smiled just a little and gave Alice a reassuring wave. Margery kept on weeping, until Julian began to wonder if the tears would ever stop. Finally, with a sequence of wet sniffles, she stopped and smiled at Julian, a single, salt tear hanging on the end of her nose.

"You see, whenever I hear the name of – of Mary, or when I think of the suffering of Jesus on the cross, I start – I break into tears…" And again, Margery began to wail and howl and sniffle.

"That's enough crying, Margery!"

Surprised, Margery pulled herself together. "I try very hard to make myself holy so I got myself a haircloth from a kiln; the kind that malt – malt is dried on and I put it on underneath my clothes and I did it secretly, of course, because I didn't want anyone, especially my hus – husband, to know."

"Then why are you telling me?"

Margery looked startled. "Well, ah – I – I want you to tell me if I am doing the right things to be holy because whenever people say nasty – nasty things about me because I weep so long and loud for my Lord's suffering, I say 'thank you' to Jesus for it and I think he is glad – glad when I bear their scorn for his sake and when God sends me temptations, I bear – bear them also."

"What temptations?"

"I saw a man in church and he came to me afterward and said he wanted so badly to – to – to go to bed with me, and Mother Julian, a wondrously handsome man he was, but I said no, of course, but then later I wanted him so badly I went – went and told him I was ready for him and you know what he did? He said he didn't want to lie – lie with an old biddy – biddy like me! He called me an old biddy, Mother Julian. He called me – me that!"

Julian took a deep breath to keep from laughing. "That wasn't the kind of scorn you wanted to bear for Jesus?"

"I desire nothing but heaven. All of the apos – apostles, martyrs, confessors and virgins, and all those who ever came to heaven, passed by the way of tribulation, and so God has commanded me to go visit priests and bishops and holy men and virgins – virgins to tell them of the grace and love that God has put into my soul and to show them how I weep for the love of Jesus."

"Do you weep as loud and as long for them as you did for me?"

"Much more so! I sometimes cry for several – several hours, and then I am exhausted."

"I don't wonder."

"So tell me, Mother Julian. You are an anchoress and a virgin so tell me if it is true that such tears – tears as mine are a gift of God."

Julian sighed. After so many years, she was just a little tired of telling people that as an anchorite she wasn't necessarily a virgin. Somewhat wearily, she explained once again. "Margery, I am not a virgin. I was married. I had two children. They died in the last pestilence. Being a virgin would not make me any wiser or any more holy. God loves you and me, and honours the children we have born, and the bodies in which they were formed. When you become pregnant with a child, it is God who creates the child in you. God commands us to be fruitful and to multiply, and God cannot and does not command us to sin. Therefore it is not sinful to lie with your husband."

"But the church teaches that it is a filthy and a dirty – dirty thing!" Margery protested.

"Some churchmen teach that. You may have heard your priest and even a bishop say that. But the great teachers of the church say otherwise. God created us out of love. You and I are part of the very body of God, and God is not complete until we are made one with God. Don't despise your body, Margery. It is God's loving creation."

Margery sniffed. "Our bodies are – are vile."

"God does not find our bodies to be vile. God's goodness reaches right down to our lowest needs. Think of it this way, Margery. You and I walk upright, and the food that we eat is sealed as in a well-made purse. When the time comes, the purse is opened and lets out the waste, and then is sealed again. God is part of that too – part of our lowest needs. After all, our bodies were created by God. How then can God despise our bodies?"

Margery was silent for a long while, an unusual state for her. This was high theology she had never encountered before. Then, in an attempt to get the conversation back to herself, she asked, "And my tears of contri – contrition and sorrow are they sent from God, as I believe they are, or are they sent by Satan as some false – false – false people say they are?"

"When you find yourself in tears, that may well be the Holy Spirit working in your soul. Real tears of sorrow at the pain of the crucifixion are given to us so that we may feel the pain and suffering that humans visit on each other, and so be more able to stand with them in their suffering. Tears are a gift of God, but like God's gift of our bodies, they can be misused."

With that, Margery again burst into tears, and subjected Julian to another session of wailing and sniffles.

When she finally stopped and was busily wiping her eyes and nose on her sleeve, Julian tried again. "Margery. Do not use your tears to impress people with your piety. If you cry too loud and too long, people will think you strange. Tears are a gift, but don't cry so long or so loud or so often. The gift of tears, like all of God's good gifts, must be used with care. Don't worry about what people say about you. That isn't important. Learn to listen to the voice of God, and then speak what you learn quietly and with great humbleness."

"Thank you, Mother – Mother Julian," said Margery, sniffling again.

"Where do you go from here?"

"I wish to go on pilgrimage, to show my devotion to Go – God and if I can find someone to give me some money, I will go to the Holy Land so that I can weep and pray on the very spot – spot where our Lord was crucified."

Once again, Julian tried to offer advice, though by now she was fairly sure that Margery didn't really hear what she had to say. "Do not try too hard to be a holy person, Margery. Those who try to show others their holiness are seldom holy themselves. Those who try to become saints always fail." Then Julian leaned close to the window and whispered loudly, "And Margery, you can't become a virgin again."

—

Margery did go to the Holy Land. Her father, John Brunham, died in early October of that year and remembered Margery in his will. That made her independently wealthy. Very shortly after that, Margery left on her pilgrimage – a remarkable journey for a woman, especially since she travelled much of the way alone. Most of the journey was on foot. The last part of the trip was on a small open boat, a frail craft against the storms that can whip the Mediterranean into a frenzy.

Margery, like most pilgrims, tried to find others travelling in the same direction. A larger group was less vulnerable to the brigands who preyed on travellers. She would tell her fellow pilgrims about her piety, and often treat them to long, sobbing, crying spells. Margery never did understand why those with whom she was travelling often left early in the morning before she was awake, or tried other tactics to be rid of her. Some refused to board the same ship with her. It seemed to Margery they were ungrateful, after she had offered them her preachments and demonstrated the quantity of her tears.

More than twenty years and several journeys later – to Canterbury, to Rome and Assisi, to Santiago de Compostela, and to Danzig – Margery began to dictate her long, rambling story to a priest who wrote it down for her. *The Book of Margery Kempe,* it is called, and it is all, very modestly, in the third person. She tells of many encounters with learned doctors, priests, and holy men of all sorts, most of whom, she says, were wonderfully impressed by her piety and her loud and copious tears. She wrote of her visit to Julian, and gives a short account of the counsel she received.

Margery was tried for heresy a few years after her visit with Julian. This was in Leicester, immediately after her return from Santiago. They accused her of being a Lollard. But Margery had neither the wit nor the imagination to be anything but totally orthodox in her beliefs. The main charge was that she was preaching, which should only be done under licence from the bishop and certainly never by a woman. "Sir," said Margery, "I have never entered a pulpit, nor do I speak in church. I simply tell people, whenever I can, of how the Good – Good Lord has spoken to me and given me tears of contrition." They let her off but told her to leave the diocese.

In the end, Margery gained at least some of the respect and attention she so deeply craved. In 1438, she was admitted to the Guild of the Trinity at Bishop's Lynn, a very high honour for a very courageous woman.

Margery (Maggie) Baxter would have been shocked and confused had she met and conversed with her namesake. She had come to see Julian every few months since her first visit more than ten years earlier.

Maggie had grown stout and matronly. The babies she so ardently prayed for had come. She openly called herself a Lollard now. Julian breathed a prayer of thanks that Margery and Maggie had not come at the same time. And she wondered what they would have done to each other.

"Do you know that Thomas à Becket?" Maggie demanded. "'Thomme of Cankerbury,' we call him." She laughed at her own joke. "They talk about how brave he was, stayin' at the altar, prayin' till the king's men came and stabbed him. It ain't true. He was runnin' scared, he was, and they caught him at the church door tryin' to get away." Maggie was loud, nervous, agitated. "You know where he is now, Sister Julian? That great Saint Thomas is fryin' in hell, he is. He gave the church cartloads of gold and silver and jewels. He made the church richer than ever. He seduced the common folk, folk like me and you, lady, tryin' to get us to believe all that clap trap about pilgrimages and given' money to the church. Ain't that somethin'?" Maggie had become much more self-confident, more articulate, more strident over the years. Julian wasn't sure if that was an improvement.

"You don't believe in pilgrimages?" Julian was never quite sure how to respond to Maggie.

"Oh, I wish you could hear my friend Hawisia Mone tell about pilgrimages, how pilgrims only make priests wealthy so they can buy fine food and wine and clothes and keep mistresses. Them stupid, benighted pilgrims make themselves poor goin' to the shrine at Walshingham. Our Lady of Walshingham, they call her. But Hawisia, she calls her 'Our Lady of Falsyngham,' And the one they call 'Our Lady of Woolpit' Hawisia she calls 'Our Lady of Foulpit.' Again, Maggie cackled at her own wit. "She's a fine one, Hawisia is. That's sure."

Lollardy was strong in East Anglia. Not so much in Norwich itself, but in the towns around it. Earsham, Seething, Beccles, Loddon, Martham (Maggie's home), and many others. Maggie and her husband William, along with Hawisia Mone and her husband Thomas, a wealthy businessman, were unabashed leaders of the sect.

How the name "Lollard" came to be, no one could say. It certainly wasn't invented by the founder of the movement, John Wycliffe. He was "a tall, thin figure, covered with a long, light gown of black colour, with a girdle about his body; the head adorned with a full flowing beard, exhibiting features keen and sharply cut; the eye clear and penetrating; the lips firmly closed in token of resolution." He also had a large hooked nose.

Wycliffe was a scholar, not a popular reformer. He excelled at academic debate in Latin; at detailed, abstract scholarly argument. John of Gaunt, the Duke of Lancaster, took an early interest in Wycliffe and became, in a sense, his patron. So also did Joan of Kent, the Queen Mother.

Wycliffe argued that the power to appoint men to church offices should belong to the king, not with the pope. It was the kind of argument the royalty loved to hear, especially from a respected, scholarly priest. The British nobility were in a constant power struggle with the church. Wycliffe provided them with carefully argued justification.

The protection of such nobles meant that even though Wycliffe was called to appear before the bishops on several occasions, they really could do nothing to him. Wycliffe argued that all faith must rest on the authority of the Bible, which should be available in English, so that all could read it. Some of his colleagues had undertaken an English translation based on the Latin *Vulgate*. The first part of that literalistic (and often rather bad) translation of the Bible was the Gospel of Luke, which Maggie had shown Julian.

But Wycliffe eventually went too far. He challenged the doctrine of transubstantiation. He claimed that the bread and the wine in the Mass were *symbols* of the body and blood of Christ. They did not actually *become* the body and blood of Christ. With that he lost the support of the nobility and earned denunciation in no less than five bulls, official proclamations from the pope.

Wycliffe, like most reformers, put words around the feelings and discomforts that many, especially those in the growing English middle class, already felt. The scholarly Oxford schoolman crystallized their antagonism toward the church. The word spread quickly that there might be another way to be faithful than that prescribed by the Roman Church.

The church reacted. In 1407, Thomas Arundel, archbishop of Canterbury, issued an edict that "nobody shall from this day forth translate any text of Holy Scripture into English...and no such English text shall be read in public or in private." And so English became the language of the religious underground.

"The priests they say that when they mumble their Latin words over the bread and wine, that it gets to be the body and blood of Jesus." Maggie Baxter was in full sail now, giving Julian a large dose of the ideas being discussed in the small groups that met at her home and the homes of many other Lollards. "Well, I say, if it's the body and blood of Jesus goin' into them folks kneelin' in front of the priests, then it's got to be the body and blood of Jesus when it comes out of their arse when they're sittin' on the thunder bucket at night doin' their business." Maggie hooted at her own wit.

Julian recoiled in revulsion. "Maggie! You have said many things to me here, and I have not argued with you. But I have been fed, I have been nursed at the breast of our Mother Jesus who is all love. When I receive the Eucharist, our beloved mother Jesus feeds us with himself. I won't have you turning this holy miracle into a crude joke!"

Maggie was chastened, but only slightly. "Did I hear you right, Julian? Sayin' that Jesus was a woman?"

"No. I said nothing of the kind." Julian paused to collect her thoughts. "Maggie, you have the children you wanted so badly."

"Oh, indeed. Four I've had. And two of 'em still alive."

"Then you know, Maggie, that when I use the word 'mother' I am talking about a way of loving. It is sweet and natural. It is the only word we can use to describe the way our Lord feeds us. A kind, loving mother knows and understands the needs of her child, and protects her child, tenderly. That's the nature of motherhood. As the

child grows older, a mother changes the way she treats her child, but she never changes her love. Sometimes she lets the child get into trouble, because that is the way a child learns. She may allow the child to fall sometimes. And sometimes she punishes the child. But she does those things in love. And so our Lord loves us in this same mothering way."

"Next thing you'll be sayin' is that God is some kind of mother."

"And you are right, Maggie Baxter. But God is not a human being like you and me, so we can't say that God is a man or a woman. Do you still believe in the Holy Trinity, or has that also been cast aside by you and your Lollard friends?"

"Oh, we honour the Trinity, for certain."

"God our Father, God almighty, is the first person of the Trinity. The second person of the Trinity is our natural mother. We are grounded and rooted in this natural mother. When God took on our human form as Jesus, when God took on our sensuality, God also became our merciful mother. And so our mother works in many different ways, helping us, nurturing us, feeding us. And grace and mercy comes to us through the third person of the Trinity, the Holy Spirit, who rewards us and gives us hope and joy. The Holy Spirit offers special hope and joy to those who are in pain or who are poor and suffering. Our essence is our father, God almighty. Our essence is our mother, God all-wisdom. And our essence is the Holy Spirit, God all-goodness. The Trinity is all one God, and all that we can know of goodness and forgiveness and love is there in that one God."

"I don't know. I don't know, Julian, but me thinks if the Bishop of Norwich heard that kind of talkin', you'd be cooked the way they've been cookin' some of our friends. I'm no schoolman, but that sounds to me like harder heresy than what us Lollards have been sayin'."

"I believe what Holy Church teaches me, Maggie. I have no reason to doubt any of it. What I have just said to you about the mothering nature of God has been said before. I have copied and read some of the books written by the church fathers. I have not said anything that they have not said before me. It was not heresy then, and it is not heresy now, even though many of today's bishops and priests would disagree strongly." Julian could see she had Maggie's full attention. She was an intelligent and courageous woman, Julian realized, even with her sometimes strange ways.

"I believe what Holy Church teaches, Maggie, but I don't always believe what some of its priests and bishops say. Some of them speak out of their greed and their lust for power. Others speak out of their fear, especially their fear of women. Did you know, Maggie, that some of them do not believe that women – you and I – have a soul? And so we don't always hear the gentle message of love and forgiveness of which our Lord spoke, and of which the fathers of the church have so often written. The priests and bishops of the church do not always teach the true nature of the Trinity. Many do not even know the gentle gospel that we hold so dear."

For a long moment the two women held each other's eyes. Then Maggie looked away and blinked back some tears she didn't want Julian to see. But she couldn't hold them back. She wept silently for a while, then turned back to Julian. "I'm sorry, Mother Julian. I do it every time. I try to be funny and then I hurt someone."

"Then why do you try to be funny?"

"Because...because I have such a burning in my belly, such a burning about how Jesus wants a church that all of us can be part of. They've been readin' the Bible in English at our meetings, even though we know it's against the church's law. And it seems so right to me that everybody – not just priests – all the folks should hear that story. Most of all, I like the story of how Jesus loved us so terrible much he let himself get strung up for us. Everybody should hear that!"

"And you are right, Maggie. God wants that too. And that is what Holy Church teaches, even though there are many – priests and bishops too – who don't know that. They need to read that story too."

"Yeah! And it's a cryin' shame!"

"Maggie." Julian's voice was kind but firm. "You must be aware that you could be severely punished for some of the things you say and do. Especially the things you said about the Eucharist. You could be burned as a heretic!"

"I know." Maggie was totally subdued now and spoke in a whisper.

"Aren't you afraid?" Julian asked.

"For sure, I'm afraid. I'm scared spitless. That's why I come on so strong tryin' to be funny. Sometimes I'm so scared I can hardly get out of bed in the morning, and sometimes I'm so fired up I've got to go out and say what God is tellin' me."

"Yes, I understand that, Margery." Julian reached through her window and took her hand. "I understand that very, very well."

"How come you called me Margery?"

"It's a better name for a woman with such courage."

"I always wanted folks to call me Margery. Nobody ever did."

"And they probably won't call you Margery now, no matter what you tell them. But you can think of yourself as Margery."

"Margery Baxter! Ain't that somethin'?"

"God be with you Margery. You will be in my prayers. And Margery, even though the world seems so full of pain and anger, and even though you may suffer for what you believe, God *can* make all things well, and God *will* make all things well. Believe that Margery. Believe that!"

Not long after her visit to Julian, Margery Baxter was arrested and tried for heresy. She was found guilty. Half-naked, in a humiliating, loose-fitting kirtle, and carrying a large candle, Margery was subjected to four floggings around Martham Church on Sundays, and two more around Acle on market days. Then she was required to pay two penitential visits to Norwich Cathedral. She was told quite clearly; "If you offend again, you will be burned at the stake."

1414

And so I saw
that God is delighted to be our father,
and God is delighted to be our mother,
and God is delighted to be our true spouse.
Christ is delighted to be our brother,
and Jesus is delighted to be our Saviour.

There was a loud thumping in the anteroom beside Julian's cell three days later. An elderly priest was banging his walking stick against the wall for attention. "I am Father John Carter and I am here at the behest of the bishop. Word has come to us that you have been talking to dangerous women at your window. What do you say?"

Julian pulled back the curtain and looked at the priest. She drew back, startled. "Have we met before, Father? I feel I know you."

"I am certain we have not," said the priest, not trying to hide his annoyance. He was large man with a distinctive nose. His robes hung loosely on a bony, once muscular frame, now stooped with age. "Stop staring at me, and tell me about these dangerous women you have been entertaining!"

"Dangerous women? Well, Father, that would indeed be entertaining. I have spoken to no one who seems dangerous, except perhaps to themselves. Who do you have in mind?"

"We are told they both came within a day of each other. Margery Kempe and Maggie Baxter. We are told they may be dangerous to the sanctity of Holy Church."

"Really? Is this the kind of speculation you amuse yourself with in the bishop's palace? Surely, you are not serious." Julian tried to look incredulous to hide the fear she suddenly felt.

"You are shut away from the realities of the world, woman. We do not have that luxury. Now tell me about these women."

"Margery Kempe is a simple soul. She would like very badly to be a virgin again, this after bearing many children. And she is trying to become a saint, though she cannot understand that those who wish to be saintly almost never are."

"It is said she cries loud and long."

"Oh, indeed. Very loud and very long. And she tells anyone who will listen how the Good Lord came to give her that gift. To some, her loud crying is an annoyance, but it is hardly a threat to the church. I have never known anyone who wants so badly to believe every bit of what the church may teach her. Margery Kempe is more orthodox than you are, Father!"

Father John scowled and Julian smiled. "And Maggie Baxter?" the priest demanded.

"Maggie has a strong, sharp tongue and speaks well, but sometimes not too wisely. Her barbed sayings sometimes outrun her good sense. But she is no threat to the church."

"Is she a Lollard?"

"If you tell me what a Lollard is, I may be able to answer your question." Julian was stalling for time.

The priest drew a long, impatient breath. "A Lollard is a follower of the heretic John Wycliffe, who preached many slanders against the church."

"We spoke not a word, either of us, about John Wycliffe." Julian knew this was a white lie and she wasn't proud of it. But she couldn't bring herself to betray Margery Baxter, even though she had clearly spoken heresies.

"And you, Julian. You have developed quite a reputation in this land. There are those who say you do not always tell others what Mother Church has taught you. On what authority do you do this?"

"I was placed in this anchorhold by Bishop Despenser, may God rest his soul. I was charged by him to lead a life of prayer and simplicity and to counsel those who came to my window in spiritual need. I pray daily that God may give me the grace to do this small task faithfully and well. It is well known that I have been given a vision of the passion of our Lord Jesus. I have reflected on that vision, meditated on its meanings all these years in this anchorhold. I do not even know how many years that has been. As you can see, I am now an old woman. This vision, this gift of Christ, is my authority to speak God's love and grace to my fellow Christians."

"How can it be that a woman understands the teachings of Holy Church enough to teach others?"

"I do not teach, Father John. I simply say to others what God has said to me. Because I am a woman, should I therefore not speak of what has been shown to me? Should I not tell of the unbounded love of God for every creature?"

"Every creature? Even heretics?

"Yes. Even heretics! God, like a loving mother, reaches out with special love to those children who have strayed or fallen." Julian could see the priest's rising agitation, but she kept on. "That is the meaning of Christ's presence here on earth, to reach out with loving hands to everyone – to save the weak and the lost. Those who are well have no need of a doctor. Those who are well have no need of an old anchorite like me. But the sick of soul come to me, and I remind them of the all-encompassing love of God. I can do nothing else."

"Woman, God is not a mother. God is a father, a judge who exacts vengeance on those who deny him. That is what you will teach!" A network of red veins spread across the priest's cheeks. He was almost shouting now. "And if anyone comes in here and utters foul heresies, you will send word of that to me immediately. Do you understand?"

Julian said nothing, but looked the priest squarely in the eye.

"Answer me woman! Do you understand?" he bellowed.

"I understand all too well. But an avenging father God was not shown to me, so I cannot speak of such a thing. Nor can I tell you what the people who come for counsel have said to me."

"You are not a priest hearing confession. You will do as you are instructed," the man hissed, "or you will be required to appear before a tribunal to answer for your disobedience."

"I will do as I am instructed by my Lord and my God. And I am confined to this anchorhold until I die."

The cleric whacked his stick against the wall and stomped out of the anchorhold, angry and defeated. He knew well that Julian was loved, admired, even venerated by the people of Norwich. There might well be riots if they dragged her from the anchorhold to face a tribunal.

Julian felt a sense of triumph. A sense of power. And then immediately regretted both emotions. She was not blind to the esteem in which she was held by the folk who came to her cell, and because of this, she was not as vulnerable to pressure. This sense of power was a new temptation to be faced, and she would need to pray hard over it.

Even so, she knew well that Bishop Tottingham, who had succeeded Bishop Despenser, could find a way to discipline her if he chose. But he was politically astute enough to choose his battles carefully. And he chose to put increasing pressure on the Lollards, now active in almost every part of his diocese.

For several days, Julian had had the angry priest and the two Margerys in her prayers. "They are so frightened, so fragile," she had prayed. "Strengthen them with your love."

But Julian could not get the face of Father John Carter out of her mind. The moment Alice placed the evening meal on the sill between their rooms, she knew. The priest reminded her of Alice. The resemblance was unmistakable.

"Alice, do you know anything at all about the circumstances of your birth?"

"No, Julian!" Alice was taken aback by the suddenness and intensity of Julian's question. "All I know is that a priest sold me to the farmer, and the farmer took me to the whorehouse. Nobody ever talked to me about nothin' then. It wasn't till I ran to the convent that I could ask any questions."

"Have you ever wondered who your parents were?"

"Sure. When I lay there in the straw beside the cows, I made myself parents in my own head. My father was a handsome prince and my mother was a beautiful princess, but they had me afore they got married so they took me to the priest. And one day, they would come lookin' for me. It was a nice dream."

"What would you do if you found out who your parents were?"

"I'd fall over in a dead faint, most likely. What are you tryin' to say to me, Julian? You know something, don't you?"

"No, I don't *know* anything, Alice. But I have a suspicion. I think I know someone who is closely related to you."

Alice sat down hard. "Jumpin' horseflies!" Beyond that she was speechless. "Jumpin' horseflies!"

Julian waited. Alice sat in stunned silence. Finally she found a voice. "All my life I've wanted a family." She spoke in a hoarse whisper. "All my life I've wanted a family."

"Alice." Julian spoke as gently as she knew how. "Finding someone who is a blood relative is not the same as finding a family. Families are about love and tenderness and caring. I know people say that bloodlines are what's important, but that isn't always true. You and I are a family, here, living in this anchorhold. You already have a family."

"Who is this person, this relative of mine, Julian?"

"Father John Carter. He came to my cell because he thought I was entertaining dangerous women."

"You think we're related?"

Julian nodded.

"Did he tell you this?"

"No, Alice. He knows nothing of this. But when I saw his face, I felt I recognized him, even though I'd never seen him before. And then later that day, when you came in the door, I saw a very strong resemblance. You and he are kin. But Alice, he is an angry, blustering cleric. If he is related to you, he is not likely to admit it."

"That's what one of the guys in the market said. A couple of months ago. He said he seen a priest that was my daddy – we were spittin' images. I told him to shut his face or I'd punch him."

"Alice! You're too old for that."

"I know. I know. So what do I do now, Julian?"

"Don't do anything. But keep your eyes open. When you go to and from the market, go a little out of your way and walk past the cathedral. Eventually you'll see him. Even from far off, you can tell if it might be him because he carries a walking stick. You'll know what to do when you see him."

It was six weeks later that Alice saw Father John Carter. On her daily trip to the market, she went out of her way to walk in the vicinity of the cathedral, and one day she saw him coming down the street toward her. Alice had studied her own face in the reflection in the rain barrel almost every day, so she knew what she looked like. Julian was right. She and this priest had to be related.

"Good morning, Father John," said Alice bowing slightly. The priest looked at her, stopped for just a moment. His face blanched, then flushed. Then looking straight ahead, he walked past her.

Alice turned to watch him go. A few dozen steps down the street, the priest turned for another look, then seeing her smiling at him through her tears, turned quickly and hurried off.

"I think he's my father," Alice said to Julian. "Leastwise, that's what I am goin' to think. Maybe he is and maybe he ain't, but I'm gonna think of him as my papa. On my way walking back here to

Saint Julian's, I started makin' up a story in my head about how he was a young priest, and he fell in love with my mama who was young and beautiful, but her parents wanted her to marry some lord or duke or somethin'. So they kept her closed up in a room till she had the baby – till she had me – and then they took me and put me on the steps of the church."

"You would have been a wonderful daughter to them," Julian smiled, "if only you'd had the chance. Are you going to try to see him again?"

Alice thought about the question. Finally she shook her head. "Nah! It would only get him all upset. He's an old man now. So maybe that's one nice thing I can do for him. I'll leave him alone."

"Another nice thing you can do for him, Alice, is to pray for him. I have no doubt he's feeling upset, seeing you on the street. And pray for your mama. You don't know who she is, but God knows. And I'll pray for you and for them too."

Alice began to tidy the room. Julian knew she'd say more when she was ready. "I guess it don't matter. If I ever see him again, I mean." There was a peacefulness about the way Alice spoke. "Maybe he's scared that his buddies in the bishop's palace will make fun of him. But I guess it's all right. Maybe it has to be all right."

Alice carried out a bundle of bruised and dirty rushes she had gathered from the floor. A moment later she was back with a clean bundle, which she began spreading. "I sure would like to see him again, y'know. But I ain't goin' to try findin' him again. I think I've seen my papa, and so I'm goin' to say thanks to God for that. At least I feel like I was born of real parents now, not found under a cabbage leaf somewhere."

Alice felt her lip tremble. She walked slowly to the open door and studied the hazelnut tree in the garden. Then she turned back to Julian. "Hey! I got me a family name now. I ain't just plain Alice no more, I'm Alice Carter. It don't make no difference to nothin', but it sure feels good."

Julian saw the tears in her old friend's eyes. "You had a terrible start in life, Alice. Nobody should have to go through what you suffered. But you have triumphed! You have become a wonderful person and a blessing to many. Especially to me."

"It sure woulda been nice to have had a family. But you keep tellin' me that God is both mother and father to me, and y'know somethin'? I'm startin' to believe you. And for sure, I've got you for a big sister."

"And all shall be well," said Julian under her breath. "And all shall be well!"

1415

Sin is inevitable.
But all shall be well,
and all shall be well,
and all manner of thing
shall be well!

ulian could not remember a winter so cold. Her small fire seemed to offer little of the warmth her old bones craved. The extra woolen cape she wrapped around herself was of small comfort. Her body, it seemed, generated too little warmth for the heavy wraps to keep inside.

But each morning she struggled out of bed, every joint and muscle protesting. She could no longer kneel – her knees would not allow it – so she would sit before the tiny fire to repeat her morning office. And every afternoon she sat at her window, ready to draw back the curtain when a voice called from outside, even though she dreaded the gust of cold air that would invade her cell. More and more, she treasured the silence, the solitude, the peace between *compline* in the evening and the beginning of the visits the next afternoon. She also understood much more profoundly how her solitude made it possible to hear what those hurting people said through her window, and how their stories, their tears and their occasional laughter became the text of her meditation and her prayers.

Julian opened her curtain to almost everyone now, even though she was roundly criticized for it, especially by some priests. "How can you know what is in a person's heart if you cannot see their face?" she would ask.

They came in a steady stream, it seemed. Old men, young women, artisans and priests, all coming to speak of their pain or fear or anger, and to hear from Julian the words of holy love she never tired of speaking. Alice, bent over and arthritic like Julian, made mugs of warm barley broth for both of them, to hold and warm their hands – to drink and warm their bellies. Each day, as winter turned to spring, the days grew longer and the world grew warmer.

"Alice," Julian stood at the window between their two rooms one afternoon when the last visitor had come and gone. Alice was preparing their light evening meal. "How long have we been together?"

Alice responded with a gap-toothed grin that wrinkled up and down her face. That generated an even more wrinkled grin from Julian. "I lost count years ago. But for sure, we're a couple of old crones. We lived longer'n most of our friends."

"Are you afraid of dying, Alice?"

"Nah! I'm lookin' forward to it. My body took a lot of whackin' when I was a kid. I can still feel every one of them bruises whenever the weather turns cold and rainy. I'll be powerful glad when God lets me bury this bag of bones and gives me a new kind of body that doesn't get such aches and pains. And – do things like this happen in heaven? I'm hopin' to see my father again. I only had just that one good look at him. And then he died a few months later. And, will I meet my mom, I wonder?"

"Did you ever tell anyone about your father? Does anyone know except you and me?"

"No. For sure I was the only family he had at his funeral mass."

"It's been quite a life you and I have lived, Alice," Julian marvelled.

"Yeah. I wonder how many folks, over all them years, came here to see you. How many do you figure? Some of them almost bleedin' they hurt so bad."

"Well, Alice, you've done your share of God's work too. I've been told there are many people who come up to you in the market and pour their hearts out to you. Often you can speak to them out of your life and experience far better than I ever could." Alice waved off the kind exaggeration. "No, it's true, Alice. They keep coming to you and to me, to be warmed at the small flame of faith that burns in us."

The two old women stood there. Alice stirred the pot of gruel she was cooking. "Lotsa memories, eh?"

"You know my favourite memory, Alice? Years ago when I was copying the Gospel of Luke, and I was telling you what it said in English. I was telling you the story of the Pharisee who invited Jesus to eat with him. And a woman from the streets came in. And you said, 'You mean a whore?' Then I told you how she put some expensive ointment on Jesus' feet – she was crying while she did it – and she was kissing Jesus' feet."

"Oh yeah! I sure remember that. That important guy got mad at Jesus and told him he shouldn't have nothin' to do with the likes of that whore. And Jesus, he says to that important guy, 'Hey, you didn't do nothin' for me when I come in. But this woman has been doin' nice things to me. Well, this woman, see, she has done lotsa wrong things, but her sins are forgiven. You maybe don't have so many sins, but you ain't got them forgiven, neither.' And then Jesus says to the whore, 'Go in peace.'"

"You saw yourself in that story, didn't you, Alice? I remember the look on your face then. It's the same look you have on your face right now."

Again, the warm and comfortable silence held between them.

"I was tryin' to figure out how many winters I'd been alive," said Alice. "I wish I had one of them lookin' glasses, where you can look into and see yourself. I seen myself in the rain barrel lotsa times, and I guess I'm a sight. Lots of wrinkles. My hair is mostly white. Haven't got more'n a few teeth left."

Julian laughed. "You are a sight, Alice. But you know, you're beautiful at the same time."

"Do you know how old you are, Julian?"

"It must be more than seventy winters, I suppose. Maybe more. I should have died long ago. My old body is so bent and so tired. Surely, soon, my little flame will be enfolded into God's holy fire. Remember when I had my showings, Alice? I had asked God to bring me close to death so that I might know what dying was like. I thought it would help me die in a way that was pleasing to Christ. It was a naïve, childish request, but God granted it anyway. I've had the rehearsal and now I think I'm ready to get on with the real thing." Suddenly Julian became serious. "When we die, we enter God's mystery, Alice. It's a well of mystery that has fed us, cared for us, sustained us whenever we went to drink of it. As we die, we enter into that loving mystery. We are born again."

Again the two old women savoured the silence between them, knowing that such words spoken from deep within the soul need time to be tasted and treasured.

After a while, Alice spoke. "Are *you* afraid of dyin', Julian?"

"Alice!" Julian chortled, "I have been officially dead all those years we forgot to count. The bishop buried me, remember? 'Earth to earth, ashes to ashes, dust to dust.'" Suddenly Julian burst out laughing. "Do you remember what you said about Bishop Despenser, Alice?"

"No. I suppose it was something awful."

"It was wonderful. 'Pinched like a bull's arse in fly season.'" Both women cackled with laughter.

"You know Alice, the best part of my life has been here, dead, in this anchorhold. This living death is like a rose with thorns. Sometimes I've been pricked so deeply the pain of this enclosure was almost more than I could bear. Sometimes the solitude has been just awful, but mostly it has been a blessing. I've lived my life with the stink of hell and the scent of heaven coming through that window from all those people who sat there and shared their lives with me. Roses with thorns, every one of them. My life has been rich and full and lively."

Julian took the trencher of gruel and the cup of ale Alice handed to her through the window. "Only once, over all those years did I break my vow and cross over that threshold, and that was when my mother was dying. But, you know, Alice, this cell has never been a prison. It hasn't been a tomb either, which is what I feared when I became an anchorite. It's been more like a womb, and I've been expecting for years to be born into a new life. All I have to do is turn up my toes, and I'm ready for whatever God has in store for me."

"Do you have any regrets?"

"No. Well, yes." A profound sadness deepened Julian's eyes. "I wish my brother Thomas had not gone on that crusade. I wish I knew what happened to him. I wish I'd been able to say something when he came back to me that day, something that would have helped him live again." Julian's aging eyes found a few more tears to shed for her brother. "Thomas wasn't just my brother, he was also my child, and perhaps when I mourn for him, I am also mourning my two beautiful children and my strong, kind Walter."

"Did you ever wish you hadn't done it – hadn't come into this anchorhold?"

"Oh yes! I have regretted it many times. You know that as well as I do, Alice. Many times, if you hadn't locked the door, or bullied me unmercifully, I would have run from this place. You kept me here, Alice. Almost every day somebody would say something to me through my window, and then I'd wish I'd had a normal life. But now that I'm older, the moment I regret it, I also rejoice at the blessing it has been for me. I never understood why God called me here, but God understood and that was enough. When all is said and done, Alice, I have no regrets. I've been expecting to die for years and I sometimes wish God would get on with it."

Alice laughed and Julian smiled. "Which of us will go first, Alice?

It should be me because I'm about ten winters older than you are."

"If you go first, I'll go and finish my days with the sisters at Carrow Abbey. But if I go first, you'll have to train a new maid."

"I haven't had a maid for years, Alice. I have had a sister, a friend, a companion. But no maid. I don't know exactly when you stopped being a maid, Alice, but I think it was when you first called me 'Julian,' instead of 'ma'am.'"

Alice was suddenly very serious. "You never really got it figured, did you, Julian? Why do rotten things happen, especially to nice folk? Why is the world such a crappy place if God loves it as much as you say?"

"No, I didn't, Alice. Sometimes I thought I understood, but I never did. Not really. Not completely. I'm more certain now than ever that everything we can ever know about God can be said in one word. Love. Love was the meaning."

Julian picked up the hazelnuts still lying on the shelf of her prayer bench even after all these years. They were polished and beautiful from the many times she had held them in her hand. "And so it doesn't matter if I don't understand. I tried so hard to work it out in my mind, to discover it in my prayers, and sometimes I thought I was very close." One of the old hazelnuts crumbled in her hand. "I still wonder if some souls really are damned forever, or whether God will overcome all evil. There are some kinds of knowledge that are too deep for us, Alice. So we need to wait, and one day in God's good time, we will know. Someday it will all be shown to us and then we will see how our small flame and God's mighty fire shall be made one. And then, all shall be well. In the meantime, we trust."

"When I run from the whoremonger all them years ago, I wouldn't have dreamed, in a thousand years, Julian, that someday I'd be an old crone listening to a flippin' anchorite say things like that, and – here's the part that's really wild – understandin' what you are talkin' about. Or at least I think I do."

"Remember the Book of Exodus we did together – it was the last book we copied, I guess, before my eyes got too bad and my hands too crippled. It was all about the children of Israel leaving slavery and going through the wilderness to the Promised Land. That's your story, Alice. And mine too, come to think of it. I guess I'm more than ready to get into that promised land. I'm more than ready."

Alice took the trencher and the cup, then looked at her old friend with intensity and love. "Good night, my friend. God's peace be with you."

"And good night to you, Alice. God's peace be with you." Julian closed the curtain between their rooms and readied herself for *compline.* It was evening, but in the long days of springtime, the sun still shone through her small oiled linen window.

Julian walked to the other window where she had given so many struggling souls the gift of love. With her finger she traced the shape of the white cross on the curtain. In her other hand she felt the smooth, round, and tiny hazelnuts in her hand.

"All shall be well," she whispered. "And all shall be well. And all manner of thing shall be well."

Julian pulled back the curtain and a breath of spring warmth came through the window and the open door of the anteroom. From the hazelnut tree, now tall and strong, a nightingale sang a sad, sweet song.

Above the new, wet grass, a crimson rose opened its shining face to the sun.

Afterword & Resources

Having written all those words, I find myself sitting here deeply moved and grateful. Here I am, in a country Julian didn't even know existed, at a computer, an electronic marvel she wouldn't even be able to imagine. I am privileged to write a book about a woman of faith, who stole her way into my soul one day. Her message is as pointed, as relevant today as it was 600 years ago.

If somehow I could ask Julian, "What are the last words that should be in my book?" I think her response would be something like this.

Forget about Ralph's words and his stories!
Forget about me and my words!
Focus on the wonder of a God
who loves you intensely,
deeply,
completely.
This love calls you to be 'oned' with God –
calls you into completeness,
wholeness –
calls you into the mothering arms of Christ.

Some Resources

There's more material about Julian of Norwich than any one person can read, much less digest. If you go to the website www.joinhands.com, you will able to find a number of resources for those who want to continue their study of Julian.

If you are new to the subject of Julian of Norwich, Sheila Upjohn is probably your most helpful author.

- *In Search of Julian of Norwich*, by Sheila Upjohn. London: Darton, Longman & Todd, Ltd., 1995.
- *Why Julian Now? A Voyage of Discovery*, by Sheila Upjohn. London: Darton, Longman & Todd, Ltd., 1997.

There are a number of translations of Julian's work. Here are four of the better ones.

- *All Shall Be Well*, a translation by Sheila Upjohn of Julian's *Showings*. Harrisburg, PA: Morehouse Publishing, 1992. Of the various translations of Julian's *Showings*, this is easily the most readable.
- *Julian of Norwich Showings*, by Edmund Colledge and James Walsh. Mahwah, NJ: Paulist Press, 1978. Regarded by some as the most scholarly translation, this book contains a good commentary on Julian, both her Short and Long texts, and a helpful concordance.
- *Revelation of Love*, by John Skinner. New York: Image Books, 1997. Also quite readable.
- *Lesson of Love*, by Fr. John-Julian, is a readable and scholarly translation. It is available through the Order of Julian of Norwich (address below).

Various commentators have published books about Julian. Two of the most useful are:

- *Julian of Norwich*, by Grace Jantzen. London: SPCK, 2000.
- *Julian of Norwich's Showings*, by Denise Nowakowski Baker. Princeton, NJ: Princeton University Press, 1994.

If you are fortunate enough to live near Norwich or can travel there, the Friends of Julian operate a fine Resource Centre right next to St. Julian's Church. You can become a "Friend of Julian" or reach the Resource Centre at Rouen Road, Norwich, NR1 1QT, England. The e-mail address is: friendsofjulian@ukgateway.net

In the USA, the Order of Julian of Norwich (Anglican) stocks books and other resources related to Julian. They can be reached at 2812 Summit Ave., Waukesha, WI, 53188. The e-mail address is: ordjulian@aol.com.

Old hands and those who have just discovered Julian can join Ralph Milton at an online chat group that has the same name as this book. It is called Julian's Cell. To become part of this discussion, go to www.joinhands.com, click on *Ralph's Resource Barrel*, and just follow the prompts.